GREEK MYTHOLOGY

4th Edition

Gods Of Ancient Greece
And The Heroic Myths
- Discovering Greek History & Mythology -

By

Nicos Walsh

Disclaimer

This document is geared towards providing exact and reliable information in regards to the topic and issue covered. The publication is sold with the idea that the publisher is not required to render accounting, officially permitted, or otherwise, qualified services. If advice is necessary, legal or professional, a practiced individual in the profession should be ordered.

- From a Declaration of Principles which was accepted and approved equally by a Committee of the American Bar Association and a Committee of Publishers and Associations.

The information provided herein is stated to be truthful and consistent, in that any liability, in terms of inattention or otherwise, by any usage or abuse of any policies, processes, or directions contained within is the solitary and utter responsibility of the recipient reader. Under no circumstances will any legal responsibility or blame be held against the publisher for any reparation, damages, or monetary loss due to the information herein, either directly or indirectly.

The information herein is offered for informational purposes solely, and is universal as so. The presentation of the information is without contract or any type of guarantee assurance.

The trademarks that are used are without any consent, and the publication of the trademark is without permission or backing by the trademark owner. All trademarks and brands within this book are for clarifying purposes only and are the owned by the owners themselves, not affiliated with this document.

Table of Contents

Chapter 14

Conclusion

Your FREE Gift

As a way of saying *thanks* for your purchase, I'm offering this **"Greek Mythology Family Tree"**

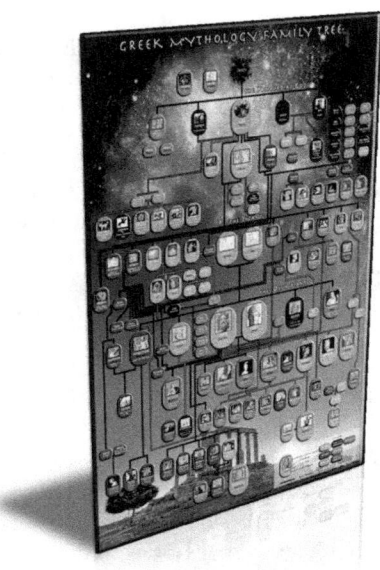

You can download this free gift by clicking here

Introduction

I want to thank you for downloading this book, "*GREEK MYTHOLOGY* - Discovering Greek History & Mythology" and hope it helps you get a deeper understanding of the intriguing Greek Myths.

The Greek civilization is considered to be the precursor of the western civilization that, one can say, has spread all over the globe today. Other cultures continue to have a strong presence in the world but they have all been westernized to a certain extent. Reason, logic, democracy, science etc. have all become global bywords. The Greeks started something that has evolved over time and has created the world that we live in today, so it is important for us to know the history and myths that ruled the Greek world during the time when civilization was born.

Greek mythology is extremely diverse and makes for a very interesting research topic. The myths and relationships surrounding each god and hero are truly remarkable. The heroes that live on in our hearts to this day, like Heracles and Achilles, had a very colorful life. Sadly, not everyone knows about all the myths and stories related to the ancient Greeks. This book tries to keep alive this rich heritage by sharing with new and old readers, the stories of the gods and heroes that shaped not just the Greek civilization but also the modern human civilization.

While reading this book you'll come across a common theme in the myths and stories of all the gods and heroes. This theme is the overthrowing of the old order and replacement with the new. In many cases it is represented by the son killing or overthrowing the father, like when Cronus castrated Uranus and then was overthrown by his own son Zeus. This theme shows the rise of civilization. The older culture that existed at the time was more cruel and barbaric in nature. The rise of the Olympians can said to be the rise of order and civilization. The older culture was assimilated into the new. Many old gods were given new identities and stories, merged with new gods, or simply forgotten and lost forever. The Greeks knew that if the old god was too big to be forgotten, it was always better to transform them into a newer version. This adaptability is the hallmark of Greek mythology.

This book is divided into 14 chapters. In the first chapter we'll talk about the myths of origin of the world, the origin of various gods and the origin of humanity itself. In chapter 2 we'll talk about the major and minor gods of Greek Mythology including the Titans and the Olympians. Chapter 3 will discuss some myths and stories related to the gods. Chapters 4 to 13 are dedicated to the mortals, the heroes of Greek mythology. And chapter 14 is all about the different beasts and creatures that roamed the world of Greek mythology. We present each character's life story and important facts and myths related to them. We also show how each character is related to other characters in the world of Greek mythology.

This book's ultimate goal is to make sure that its readers have a grasp on the facts and fiction surrounding ancient Greece, the Titans, the gods, heroes and everything else that Greek mythology is known for. But before we begin, let's talk a little bit about the history of Ancient Greece because this is the world out of which the myths emerged and understanding it will help you better understand the myths.

Ancient Greece

The Archaic Period of the Greek Civilization is said to have begun in the 8th century B.C. This period is considered to be the beginning of Greek Literature with the works of Homer and Hesiod. But the Greek myths were created long before the 8th century B.C. The period from 12th to 8th century B.C. is known as the Greek Dark Ages and the myths might have been created even before that. Pottery from this period contains geometric drawings representing these myths. It is believed that all of these myths were handed down from generation to generation through oral poems.

It is hard to pinpoint the exact time when the myths and stories were created. For example, some of the stories about the mortal heroes are based in Mycenaean Greece, during the last of the Dark Ages. It is more likely that these stories were created and built upon over the ages and so are a work of collective authorship.

These myths are important because they help us understand the way the ancient Greeks thought. They are one of the earliest attempts by man to try and understand the universe and how it works. As the Greek civilization is considered to be the origin of modern western civilization, which has now spread all over the world and for the first time has created a truly global culture, it is important and interesting to know the earliest thoughts which led to the growth of this powerful civilization.

Mythology

Among the sources of Greek mythology two epic poems by Homer, *Iliad* and *Odyssey* are the earliest. The Homeric Hymns are also important sources but despite the name, they were not written by Homer. They are choral hymns belonging to the Lyric age. Another important source is Hesiod's *Theogony* which talks about the creation of the world, the origin of the gods and the Titans. His other poem, *Works and Days*, mentions the myths of Prometheus and the Five Ages.

Later Greek Literature includes works of historians such as Herodotus and geographers such as Strabo. Apart from these written works we have a lot of archeological evidence that tells the stories about the ancient Greeks and their gods and myths. These stories are sometimes contradictory to each other but by taking them together we can accumulate an overall image of the mythology surrounding the Greek civilization. In this book we haven't mentioned all alternate theories about every myth but have used the most popular ones for the sake of simplicity and readability.

Greek mythology can be divided into four broad periods:

- The age of gods or the origin myths

- The age when gods and humans mingled freely

- The heroic age where gods did not interfere that much in human events

- The Trojan war and stories after the war

Let us begin by talking about the origin myths.

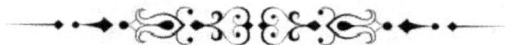

Chapter 1

The Origin Myths

The Origin Myths

The Origin of the World

In the very beginning there was nothing except Chaos, a primordial being that embodies the nothingness out of which everything in the universe emerged. For an infinitely long period of time nothing but Chaos existed. It was formless because there was no space where a form could exist. Then somehow this primordial being gave birth to 2 children.

These children were Erebus and Nyx. Erebus was the personification of darkness. He is described as the unfathomable depth where death dwells. Nyx was the personification of night. So nothingness gave birth to darkness and night. Everything else was black, silent and empty.

Then came love, or Eros. It's a miracle that out of nothingness, darkness and night should appear love. When Eros was born, order and beauty began to dispel the darkness and disorder of Chaos. Eros created light and day and with it, the earth was born as well. She was called Gaia, the mother earth. Tartarus was another child of Chaos. He was a deep abyss which was later used as a dungeon to imprison various characters including the Titans.

Gaia then gave birth to Uranus, the sky, who became the protector and partner of Gaia, surrounding it on all sides. Gaia also gave birth to Pontus, the sea, and Ourea, the mountains. With Uranus, Gaia gave birth to the 12 Titans, 3 Cyclopes, the one eyed ones, and 3 Hecatonchires, the hundred handed ones.

The Origin of the Titans

Uranus was a bad father and was displeased with his children. He felt that the Hecatonchires and the Cyclopes were monstrous and banished them into the depths of Tartarus. He was even displeased with the Titans for some reason and forced them back into Gaia's womb.

This enraged Gaia and she shaped a diamond sickle with the intention of castrating Uranus. She sought the help of the Titans. The youngest and most ambitious of the Titans, Cronus agreed to help her. Uranus was set up by Gaia and ambushed by Cronus who severed his genitals while his brothers held down Uranus. The blood that spilled onto earth caused the rise of the Giants, the Erinyes (the avenging furies), the Meliae and the Telchines. Uranus' genitals fell in the sea and from the foam came forth the Olympian, Aphrodite (Greek goddess of love).

The Origin of the Olympians

With the defeat of Uranus, Cronus became the ruler of the universe. Cronus married his sister Rhea and gave birth to the Olympians. But Gaia had prophesized that he too would be overthrown by his own son like he had done to his father. Afraid, Cronus made it a habit to swallow all his children as soon as they were born.

Rhea was displeased by this and hid baby Zeus, her sixth child and instead gave Cronus a stone wrapped in a blanket which he swallowed thinking it was Rhea's child. Zeus was raised by nymphs on the island of Crete. When he grew up he plotted to release his siblings from his father's stomach. Gaia helped him by providing him a potion. He then tricked Cronus into drinking the potion that made him vomit all of his children out.

Titanomachy

Zeus's siblings were freed but Cronus was still alive. He decided to fight against the Olympians and gathered all of the Titans. All except Prometheus, Epimetheus and Oceanus, joined Cronus in his fight. This war between the Titans and the Olympians is called the Titanomachy. The Titans were led by Atlas, the strongest of the Titans and the brother of Prometheus. The Olympians were led by Zeus. It would have been impossible for Zeus and the Olympians to defeat the Titans on their own, so Zeus sought help.

He went to Tartarus and freed Cyclopes and the Hecatonchires. The Cyclopes gave gifts to the Olympians. They gave Zeus the thunderbolt, to Hades they gave the helm of invisibility and to Poseidon they gave the trident. Prometheus also joined the Olympians and fought against the Titans. He did this because he had excellent foresight and he knew that Zeus would win.

The Titanomachy was such a severe war that at one point, all of creation was under the threat of being destroyed. The Olympians and their allies were just as strong and powerful as the Titans but they needed to end the war quickly in order to preserve the world.

Zeus lured the Titans into an ambush where the Hecatonchires threw huge boulders with each of their hundred hands. The Titans were overwhelmed by this barrage of boulders that were so huge that they thought that they were full sized mountains. They retreated and subsequently lost the war.

As punishment, Zeus locked the Titans in Tartarus and to Atlas, their leader in war, he gave a special punishment: to hold the entire universe on his shoulders for the rest of eternity. Zeus became the king of gods and the Olympians became the major gods residing on Mount Olympus.

The Origin of Man

There are two popular origin myths for how men came to be. But before we talk about them, let's describe the earth as the Greeks saw it. They thought that the earth was a flat circular disc. The earth was divided into two equal parts by the sea. This was the Mediterranean Sea. They were also familiar with the Black Sea and called it the Axine, the unfriendly sea, in the beginning but later it changed it to Euxine, the friendly sea. Both these seas together divided the earth into two equal parts.

Surrounding the earth on all sides was the river Ocean. Some believe that this was the Atlantic Ocean. They believed that the Ocean was a calm river that was never disturbed by waves or wind. Beyond the river was a mysterious land that they knew little about. They believed that the Cimmerians lived there but that no human had found exactly where they lived. It was thought impossible to reach the other shore by land or sea and only great heroes could find the way to reach there.

The Hyperboreans also lived across the Ocean river to the north. They were so far north that they were even beyond the place from where the north wind blew. They were happy people without much suffering and the Muses lived near them. To the south lived the Ethiopians who were so fortunate that the gods dined with them during the banquets. Across the river was also a place where those who had never committed any sins, went after death and lived in peace for eternity.

Now that the stage is set for the appearance of mankind, let's talk about the two myths of mankind's origin.

The Myth of Prometheus

In the first myth, after Zeus had defeated the Titans, he gave Prometheus, the Titan who had fought for him, the responsibility to create man. Prometheus created man in the image of the gods, from mud and Athena breathed life into it. Prometheus asked his brother Epimetheus to give gifts to all creatures on earth.

Prometheus means forethought but Epimetheus means afterthought and he was inclined to act without thinking so he gave all the good gifts such as agility, strength, speed etc. to the animals. He had nothing left to give to man. Prometheus cared about men more than he cared about Zeus and the Olympians. So he went to the sun and lit a torch and brought the gift of fire for the men. It was better than other forms of protection that the animals had.

Zeus was not happy that Prometheus had made men in the image of the gods and furthermore had given them the gift of fire, something that was reserved only for the gods before that.

He commanded that men had to make animal sacrifices to please the gods and that a portion of the sacrifice would be given to the gods. Prometheus again came to the rescue of mankind and sacrificed an ox and made two piles. In one pile he hid all the good meat inside the hide of the ox and poured the entrails over it to make it look unappealing. In the other pile he hid the bones and covered it with the fat to make it look shining and appealing. He asked Zeus to choose a pile and Zeus was tricked into choosing the pile of bones and fat. Since then man had the right to all the meat and only the fat and bones were burned at the altars of the gods.

Zeus was infuriated and decided to punish both mankind and Prometheus. He created the first woman, Pandora, and gave her exquisite beauty that no god or man could resist. He also gave her a chest full of all the evils in the world. He sent Pandora as a gift to Epimetheus who was living with the men. Prometheus had warned him not to take any gifts from Zeus but his brother couldn't resist Pandora's beauty. Pandora was told never to open her chest but since she was extremely curious she opened it and let out all the evils of the world and set them on mankind.

Zeus punished Prometheus by having him tied to stones in the Caucasus with unbreakable chains. An eagle tormented him by feeding on his liver everyday. Every night the liver grew back and Prometheus had to endure this torture everyday till Heracles finally freed him.

The Five Ages of Men

The second myth about the origin of man says that the gods created five different ages of men. The first age was the Golden Age. In this age, men were almost like gods except for the immortality part. They had no suffering and didn't have to work at all. Food grew automatically in abundance and they had great flocks of animals. They were loved by the gods and never suffered their wrath. Their deaths were also peaceful and they lived on as immortal spirits to protect later ages of men.

The second age was the Silver Age in which men had long lives but didn't have enough intelligence. They had to do work to survive but were so unintelligent that often killed each other in accidents. When they died, their spirits did not live on like those of the golden age.

The third age was Bronze Age in which tough men were formed. They were strong and vicious and this led to their downfall. They fought too many wars and led too many conquests till they all killed each other and the race died out.

The fourth age was the Heroic Age in which all the heroes and adventurers lived. These were fabulous men, sometimes as strong as gods, who lived great adventurous lives. These heroes are the ones like Heracles, Theseus and Achilles who were immortalized in stories forever. The heroes were given a beautiful garden to rest for all eternity after their death.

The fifth and final age was the Iron Age. In this age men were greedy and weak. They lived in evil times and their nature had evil deep within them. They had to work and toil a lot, just to survive and their lives were never without sorrow and suffering. This is the age of men that continues to live today. It is said that when every man and woman has forsaken god, Zeus will destroy this age of men as well.

These are the origin myths of Greek mythology that explain the origin of every god and natural phenomena as well as the origin of mankind. In the next chapter we'll talk about the individual gods one by one.

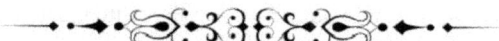

Chapter 2

The Gods

The Gods

The Titans

The Titans were the children of Uranus and Gaia. The first generation of Titans had 12 giant deities. Their children form the second generation of Titans and are 15 in number. The Titans had incredible power and strength and they ruled the Golden Age. According to Greek mythology, during the Golden Age peace and prosperity was widespread. The people were good willed and no one committed any crimes. There was no reason for pandemonium or chaos.

They were the first gods of Greek mythology, born from and later overthrowing the primordial deities that were themselves born out of Chaos. This motif was repeated when the children of the Titans, the Olympians, overthrew the Titans to become the major gods of the Greek world.

The 12 Titans were:

1. **Cronus**: Cronus was the youngest and most ambitious among the Titans. He is usually depicted with the diamond sickle that he used on his father. It became his symbol of power.

2. **Rhea**: Rhea was the sister wife of Cronus and was considered the mother of the first generation of Olympians. Rhea did not have a strong cult or dedicated followers except on the island of Crete where she was worshipped because she hid Zeus in Crete. Rhea is shown on a throne surrounded by two lions, on a chariot drawn by two lions, or simply riding a lion. The pair of lions is considered to be the symbol of Rhea.

3. **Oceanus**: Before the Olympian Poseidon, Oceanus was the sole personification for all the oceans in the world. Oceanus was the river that ran along the circumference of the earth. Later he was associated with the Atlantic Ocean while Poseidon was considered to rule the Mediterranean Sea. In most forms of art he was portrayed as having the lower body of a serpent while the upper half was human with a long beard and horns. Oceanus was not known for conflict. He did not participate in Cronus' rebellion against their father, Uranus, and later during the Titanomachy he again chose to be neutral instead of fighting for either Cronus or Zeus. This is probably the main reason why Zeus let him keep his domain after the fall of the Titans.

4. **Tethys**: Tethys married her brother Oceanus. She bore their children who were called Oceanids. Her involvement during the Titanomachy remains blurry. However, she is known to have raised the Olympian goddess Hera as her stepchild during that period. Hera was given to her by Rhea. We can see how powerful she was when she doomed the constellations, namely Ursa Major and Ursa Minor to forever roam the skies just to please her stepchild, Hera.

5. **Hyperion**: Hyperion can be translated as "the high one" and is regarded as the embodiment of light, watchfulness and wisdom. He was also personified as one of the pillars that hold the heavens and the earth apart. He was most likely to have been the Eastern pillar. It is said that he was the first one to understand the movement of the sun and the moon and the fact that they affect the changes in the seasons and so is called the father of these heavenly bodies.

6. **Theia**: Theia is also called Euryphaessa which translates as "wide-shining." She is the sister wife of Hyperion and considered to be the personification of light. She was regarded a deity of commendable beauty. She is the mother of Helios (the sun), Eos (the dawn) and Selene (the moon). She was also believed to have imparted silver, gold and the gems with their luster and radiance. She is sometimes also related to glory and victory in war or games.

7. **Coeus**: Coeus was the god of intellect and inquisitiveness. He wasn't a very familiar face in Greek mythology and makes appearances very sparingly throughout the course of Greek history. He personified one of the four pillars that held the heavens and the earth apart. He was the north pillar in that arrangement. He was involved in the Titanomachy and was banished to Tartarus when the Titans lost. Later he was overcome by madness and broke all his chains and tried to escape from Tartarus but was stopped by Cerberus, the guard dog of Hades.

8. **Phoebe**: Phoebe was the Titan endowed with the title Oracle of the Delphi. She was also called the goddess of prophecy. Her spouse was her sibling, Coeus, with whom she bore Leto and Asteria who were second generation Titans. Leto bore Apollo and Artemis who were alternatively known as Phoebus and Phoebe after their grandmother. The twins were said to have inherited their prophecy skills from their grandmother. Coeus was the intellect and Phoebe was the instinct and together the couple represented the way the human brain works. Phoebe was not involved in the Titanomachy at all and was spared punishment in Tartarus.

9. **Mnemosyne**: Mnemosyne was the goddess of memory and the word mnemonic comes from her. She is important in Greek Mythology because legend has it that Zeus slept with her for nine consecutive nights. This led to the birth of the nine Muses; Calliope (Epic Poetry), Clio (History), Euterpe

(Music), Erato (Lyric Poetry), Melpomene (Tragedy), Polyhymnia (Hymns), Terpsichore (Dance), Thalia (Comedy) and Urania (Astronomy). She was also associated with a river in the underworld that flowed parallel to the Lethe. The souls that didn't want to remember their past life upon reincarnation drank from Lethe. Those who drank from the river Mnemosyne instead became orphic poets in the next life, remembering things from the past life.

10. **Crius**: Crius is the Titan about which the least is known. Sometimes it seems that he was used just to complete the list of 12 Titans as opposed to the 12 Olympians. But Hesiod might have favored him as the father of Perses and the grandfather of Hecate. Crius took Eurybia (daughter of Gaia and Pontus) as wife. In that marriage he had three children; Pallas, Perses and Astraios. Crius was one of the four pillars that held the heavens and the earth apart. He personified the southern pillar.

11. **Themis**: Themis was the goddess responsible for maintaining undisputed order and divine right. She framed the rules and guidelines that governed men and gods. These rules were above even the gods themselves. She also had the ability to see into the future and was considered one of the Oracles of Delphi. Zeus took her as his second wife, a marriage that helped him stabilize his position over all gods and men alike. Zeus and Themis had a lot of children including the Horae and Astraea. Some believe that the Moirai or The Fates were also born from the wedlock of Zeus and Themis. Themis was related to custom, tradition, divine law and social mores rather than what was right and wrong. Her daughter Dike or in Roman, Justitia, is the one known as Lady Justice and usually shown with the scales of justice and a double edged sword. In the 16th century a blindfold was added to Lady Justice to show that justice is blind. Although Themis is the divine law, she is not the punisher and is not wrathful. It is Nemesis that brings retribution to those who disregard Themis.

12. **Iapetus**: Iapetus was considered to be a god of craftsmanship and mortality. He is personified as one of the pillars that held the heavens and earth at bay. He was the western pillar. He is supposed to have married Clymene or Asia, a daughter of Oceanus and Tethys. He had four sons, Atlas, Prometheus, Epimetheus and Menoetius. His four sons are considered to be the forefathers of the human race. Each of them had certain qualities that have passed on to the humans. Prometheus was sly and cunning, Epimetheus was foolish and stupid, Atlas had too much courage and Menoetius was arrogant and violent. These are all qualities that humans have and often lead to both their ascent and fall in life.

Zeus

Zeus was the king of gods. He was the youngest of the children of Cronus and Rhea; the sixth child. He overthrew his father Cronus and defeated the Titans in the Titanomachy and banished them to Tartarus. To save Zeus from Cronus, Rhea managed to smuggle him to a cave on Mount Ida in Crete after he was born. There are various legends as to how he was raised. Some of the popular ones are as follows:

- He was fostered secretly by Gaia.
- A goat called Amalthea took him under her care along with the Kouretes. These soldiers danced and made a ruckus with their swords and shields to prevent Cronus from hearing the cries of baby Zeus.
- Cronus had command over the earth, the heavens and the sea. So a nymph named Adamanthea raised Zeus by leaving him suspended from a tree. In this way he wasn't a part of any of his father's domains and therefore remained undetected.

After the glorified battle between the old and new gods, the victorious Olympians decided to draw lots for the domains they had to rule over. Zeus got the sky and the air. The primordial goddess Gaia was displeased with the way Zeus had treated her children, the Titans. She sent out monsters Typhon and Echidna to vanquish Zeus. Zeus triumphed over them and continued his reign.

He is considered the mightiest of all gods. In fact he was mightier than all the gods and deities put together. He ruled the sky and commanded over the clouds. He was called the rain god and his weapon was the thunderbolt, given to him by the Cyclopes when he freed them from Tartarus. Despite being so mighty, he wasn't omnipotent and all knowing like the more modern gods. He had his flaws and could be duped by others. He also didn't have any power over fate.

Zeus married his sister Hera. He was infamous for his erotic escapades and is known to have many kids apart from those Hera bore for him. His kids through Hera were Ares, Eileithyia, Hebe, Hephaestus, Angelos and Eris. He also fathered Dionysus through the mortal, Semele. He fathered the famous Greek hero, Heracles through the mortal, Alcmene. He used a nymph called Echo to distract Hera and to keep her from discovering his erotic escapades.

This created a double image of Zeus. On one hand he was the mightiest of all gods who demanded sacrifice and moral virtue from men. On the other hand he was a lustful god always cheating his wife and consummating with just about anyone. Some scholars believed that Zeus was created by merging many other gods. Whenever this new god spread to a new town, the most powerful local god was merged with Zeus. This is why it seems like Zeus had so many wives.

Zeus's weapon was the thunderbolt. His breastplate was the aegis. The eagle represented him among birds and the oak tree was his tree. His oracle was Dodona. The rustling of the leaves of the oak tree revealed the will of the god to the priests.

Hera

Hera was one of Zeus' three sisters. Zeus chose her for a spouse and she was made the Queen of the gods. She was the personification of marriage and the goddess of married women. The lion, cow and peacock were regarded sacred to her. She was infamous for her wrath. Especially towards the unfortunate women her husband slept with. Zeus' offspring were not spared from this goddess' wrath either. She does not hesitate to shower curses upon those who helped her husband by hoodwinking her while he was involved in erotic pursuits.

According to various accounts, Hera was the eldest daughter of the Titans Cronus and Rhea. Like with her other siblings except for Zeus, she was swallowed by her father until Zeus was able to free them. Zeus took his father's throne and Hera was raised by Oceanus and Thetis until the time when she married Zeus without knowing Zeus was her brother. Other accounts claim that Hestia was the eldest daughter of Cronus.

In Arcadian versions, Hera was raised by Temenus who was the son of Pelasgus. The Argive version states she was brought up by Euboea, Prosymna and Acraea, the three daughters of the River god Asterion. The Olen version states that it was the Horae who raised her. Various cities stated they were the birthplace of the goddess, including Argos and Samos, where major cult centres of Hera were established.

In addition, several cities claimed they were the location where the two Olympians had their marriage. This included Euboea, Samos, Knossos and Mount Thornax. At her wedding, Hera was gifted a beautiful golden tree that bore golden apples by Gaia. The goddess placed it in the care of the Hesperides who looked after Hera's gardens.

This appears to be a later addition as none of the Homeric works mentions it. It is only after she marries Zeus that she is given the same prestige and respect that her husband enjoys. Homer states that Zeus would listen to her advice on important matters and confided all his secrets to her. Hera feels justified in censuring Zeus when he shares information to the other gods instead of her. Despite this, however, she is completely inferior to him and is expected to obey him without question. If she doesn't, as with the rest of the gods, then she is to be punished by him. Hera is then, at least in Homeric versions, simply the wife of the king on high, and not a Queen of the gods. The notion of Hera a Queen of the Gods and wielding immense power similar to that of Zeus was not apparent until a much later time, as was possessing the gift of foresight a later addition.

Homer describes Hera as a jealous and unkind goddess in his works, with an argumentative and arrogant personality which occasionally makes Zeus tremble in fear. It is here that we first see numerous arguments arise between Zeus and Hera; at one time Hera even plotted so far to chain her husband up, helped with Poseidon and Athena. In these early instances, Zeus discovered her plots, caught her and beats her. One myth tells how he bound her hands and dangled her from the clouds with two heavy anvils weighing her down. Because of this, Hera became frightened of Zeus' temper and when he was furious she would give into him. She had to rely on her cunning and scheming nature to get what she wanted. Aphrodite would lend Hera her magic girdle in order to seduce Zeus by whom she was the mother of Ares, Hephaestus and Hebe.

Hera was the goddess of marriage and was the only Olympian to actually be married (the marriage of Aphrodite and Ares can hardly be taken seriously) and was also the goddess of childbirth. Numerous titles and epithets are ascribed to her in this nature, including Eileithuia and Teleia etc. In *The Iliad*, Homer goes on to describe her clothing and that she was driven in a chariot pulled by two horses; these creatures were harnessed and unharnessed by the Horae and her daughter Hebe. She frequently spent time in Argos, her patron city, Mycenae and Sparta.

Hera features in many of the major myths, including the Trojan War. At a wedding, the goddess of strife, Eris, threw the apple of discord into the midst which said 'to the fairest'. Hera, Aphrodite and Athena all believed it should go to them and asked Zeus to decide on the winner. Zeus wisely did not answer but gave the task of deciding a winner to Prince Paris of Troy. Each of the goddesses tried to bribe him and eventually he chose Aphrodite who promised to give him Helen, the most beautiful girl in the world. Because Paris chose another goddess over her, Hera hated the Trojans and was firmly on the side of the Greeks.

In *The Iliad,* Hera was wounded by Heracles' arrows and she asked the sun god Helios to drop down into the sea when Patroclus was killed by Hector. In *The Odyssey*, she was the patron goddess watching over Jason.

Hera was honoured all over Greece, frequently alongside her husband. Her worship goes back centuries, right into the early ages of Greece's history where she holds the surname of Pelasgis at Iolocus. She fought over the possession of Argos with her brother Poseidon but the river gods judged that it belonged to her. Her most revered temple was located at the base of Mount Euboea where statues of the three Charites was held in the vestibule. In addition, it was meant to have contained the bed of the goddess and a shield that Menelaus brought back from Troy. In Argos, the people celebrated her at the quinquennial festival. Herodotus explains in his works that Hera wasn't imported from Asia Minor (modern day Middle East) unlike that of the other Olympians and even scholars tracing the origins of her name mostly agree that Hera was most likely an original Greek deity.

Hera was no doubt an important goddess from Greek mythology; in historical terms, she appears to have been worshipped as the representation of the atmosphere whilst others believe her to be either the queen of the heavens, the stars or the moon.

Depictions of Hera show her to be a beautiful, majestic woman with wide eyes and a solemn expression on her matured face. She would typically be shown wearing a crown or diadem with a veil trailing behind to indicate her status as wife of Zeus.

Poseidon

Poseidon was the Olympian god who ruled over the seas and the second son of Cronus and Rhea. He is similar to the Titan Oceanus but they rule different domains entirely. After the Titanomachy, the big three comprising of Zeus, Poseidon and Hades drew lots to decide who gets which domains. Since no god could take over the earth as a whole, they split up whatever duties were at their disposal. Poseidon landed the seas as his domain. As a result he is called the god of the sea.

Some texts claim that Rhea managed to conceal Poseidon among some colts and scammed Cronus to swallow a colt. This theory lacks enterprise and is almost ruled out by now.

With respect to the earth, Poseidon came to be known as the "Earth-shaker" because he was responsible for causing earthquakes. His affinity for horses was well known. Poseidon was known for having a string of lovers from both sexes. His consort was Amphitrite. He was also known to have fathered many heroes like Theseus, Cercyon etc.

The earliest references to Poseidon are from the works of Homer, where he is regarded as an equal of Zeus in dignity but physically weaker. Because of this, we often see Poseidon furious when Zeus tries to intimidate him – the majority of the time the myths tell that he is submissive to his younger brother and gives into his commands, but there are times when he defies him, even going so far as to plot against Zeus with Hera and Athena. The Greeks were seamen and so Poseidon was as important for them as Zeus.

Poseidon lived in a palace in the depths of the ocean close to Aegae in Euboea. Here he looked after his horses that would pull his chariot all over the sea, the waters becoming still as he rode forward. The sea creatures, including sea monsters, would frolic around his chariot. Myths tell that Poseidon typically harnessed his horses by himself but his wife, Amphitrite, would occasionally help. Poseidon may have lived in the depths of the ocean but he would appear in Olympus as part of the assembly.

With Apollo, Poseidon is said to have erected the impregnable walls of Troy for King Laomedon but the Trojan king refused to offer the reward he had originally promised, threatening them instead. Poseidon sent a giant sea serpent to devour the king's daughter but it was killed by Heracles.

Like Hera, Poseidon then became a firm supporter of the Greeks over the Trojans and even went so far at times to actively engage in the fight, spurring the Greeks on in the guise of a Greek hero, whilst Zeus supported the Trojans. Later on in *The Odyssey*, the Greek hero Odysseus blinds Poseidon's son, the Cyclops Polyphemus, so Poseidon prevents him from returning home to Ithaca.

As the ruler of the sea, Poseidon was often depicted as bringing the clouds together and creating storms, yet he could guarantee safe passages and rescue those who were in peril. His title *gaieochos* refers him as a deity who encompasses the earth, indicating that the Greeks believed the sea surrounded the earth.

Poseidon's credit for creating the horse is like so: Poseidon and his niece were debating about as to who should have control over the capital city of Attica when it was agreed that the one who could create the most beneficial gift for the inhabitant's would be given the control over the city. Poseidon shook the ground and fashioned the horse. Athena then struck the ground and formed the olive tree. Because the olive tree could produce both food and oil, Athena was given control of the city, from then on named Athens in her honour. Other ancient writers claim that Poseidon created the horse in Thessaly and gifted them to Peleus.

The trident was the sign of the sea god, which he used to destroy rocks, call or calm storms and even cause earthquakes. Herodotus claims that Poseidon was exported to Greece from Libya although scholars believe that he was most likely a Pelasgian god (a prehistoric people from Greece and Asia Minor), and the manifestation of the nourishing power of water. Thus the transition to a sea god was quite natural.

Poseidon and Amphitrite together had three children; Triton, Benthesikyme and Rhode. But just like his brother Zeus, he had many affairs and fathered numerous children with other goddesses and human women.

Hades

Hades was the ruler of the underworld, the son of Cronus and Rhea and the brother of Zeus and Poseidon. He wasn't included among the Olympians because he resided in the underworld and hardly ever visited Olympus or the earth. He ruled over the dead but was also known as the god of wealth and in this form he was called Pluto. This is because precious metals are hidden in the earth, in his realm.

He was given a helm by the Cyclopes that made the wearer invisible. Later writers also gave him a bident. He was a terrible and unforgiving god but not an evil one. It is important to note that even though he ruled over the dead he wasn't the god of death. That position was given to Thanatos, a personification of death.

He kidnapped Persephone, the daughter of his sister Demeter, and made her his wife and the queen of the underworld. The underworld itself was known by the name of its ruler. The Greeks were even scared of uttering his name and so came up with several epithets for him like Pluto (wealthy), Agesander (one who carries away men), Clymenus (notorious), Polydegmon (who receives many), Eubuleus (good counsel) etc.

Hades was not worshipped directly but sacrifices were made to him. The Greeks were afraid of him and almost loathed him for they never wanted to meet him. Apart from the myth of Persephone's abduction, there is a myth in which Hades captured the heroes Theseus and Pirithous when they tried to steal Persephone from him. Later Heracles freed Theseus but Pirithous remained in the underworld.

Demeter

Demeter was the daughter of Cronus and Rhea and the sister of Zeus. Widely known as the goddess of harvest she also had the role of ruling over sacred law and was also responsible for the cycle of life and death. Her greatest contribution to mankind was agriculture, to be specific for cultivating cereals. Persephone was her daughter. Demeter's most famous myth concerns the rape of her daughter, Persephone, by her brother Hades. We'll talk about it in detail in the next chapter.

Demeter was a goddess of the earth but more specifically, she was the personification of the fruitfulness of the earth and later extended to agriculture where Homer names bread to be the gift of Demeter. As the manifestation of the fertility of the earth, it was further extended so that she would be a goddess of fertility in general and of marriage. The priestesses in her service would initiate young brides into what was expected of them in their new roles.

The myth about how humanity came to learn about agriculture is also related to Demeter. During her mournful wandering on earth in the search of Persephone, she met Metanira, wife of Celeus of Eleusis, as an old woman. Metanira took Demeter to her home and asked her to be the nurse of her young son Demophon. Demeter liked Demophon and decided to make him immortal. She would give him ambrosia and nectar and burn his body in the fire at night to destroy the mortal bits. One night Metanira saw this and screamed. Demeter got angry and did not make Demophon an immortal. When Metanira realized that the old woman was goddess Demeter she was inconsolable about her mistake. Celeus built a temple for Demeter and she resided there during the 9 years that she spent away from Olympus. When Persephone came back to her, she taught Metanira's other son Triptolemus, the secrets of agriculture.

Demeter was worshipped throughout Greece and locations in Sicily, Italy and Asia Minor. Her temples were named Megara and although we have an abundance of artworks representing her likeness, there is only a single statue of the goddess which has survived from antiquity. Like Hera, she is shown as a beautiful mature woman with wide eyes but with a gentler expression. She would be shown wearing a garland of corn, holding a sceptre or a torch and basket.

Athena

Athena was a very diverse Olympian exercising domain over intellectual pursuits. She was considered the goddess of inspiration, courage, wisdom, strategic war, mathematics, arts, crafts and other academic talents. She was always known to be a shrewd and cunning companion to many heroes as they went on dangerous quests. The wisest bird of them all, the owl, was Athena's sacred animal.

Some scripts cite Athena's presence much before that of Zeus. The widely accepted version states that Zeus slept with Métis. There was a prophecy that claimed that the resulting offspring would be more powerful than her father. To prevent this, Zeus swallowed Métis but she was already pregnant. Following this, Zeus began to get growing headaches. His sons cleaved his head and from there Athena sprang out already fully grown and armed.

Another version of her birth states that she was the daughter of Pallas, a giant with wings. He then tried to seduce her but she killed him instead and then used his skin and fashioned it into her aegis and placed his wings at her feet.

A third legend originating from Libya claims that Athena was the daughter of Poseidon and Tritonis. Herodotus tells that she became furious with Poseidon and went to Zeus who then adopted her as his own child. This version highlights that the Greek myths were transported to Libya from Greece and were then believed to be the originators of the Greek versions. The Libyan version tells that she was raised by Triton, a river deity, alongside his daughter Pallas. In Libya, she was regarded as the inventor of the flute.

Because of the connection between Athena and Triton and Tritonis there arose many towns and cities that would claim to be the goddess's place of birth, and wherever Triton was worshipped she was claimed to have been born there. At these locations she was known as Tritogeneia, but scholars believe it may have originated from the Cretan word trito which meant 'head', thus calling her the goddess born from the head. In connection with Triton, it seems as though her earliest worship was along the River Triton in Boetia where two Pelagian towns named Athenae and Eleusis were submerged by a lake. It is from here that her cult was imported to Greece, Libya and Asia Minor.

If we consider Athena as a daughter of Zeus and Metis, which was probably the version that was most widely accepted, then we can begin to see her status amongst the other gods. As a daughter of the most powerful god and the wisest goddess in the pantheon, Athena was a striking combination of the two. She was a harmonious combination of power and intellect and this notion led her to be one of the most popular deities in the ancient world. Ancient writers portray her to be a deity of good moral standing (unlike that of other gods) and the representation of such ethics instead of any specific natural state. She was the guardian of the country and of public organizations.

As the guardian of agriculture, Athena was accredited with the creation of the rake and plough; she created the olive tree in a contest between Poseidon and herself for control over Athens and won it (Poseidon created the horse), she trained men to yoke the ox to the plough, ensured that the horses reproduced and taught people to use the bridle on these creatures, another item she fashioned.

Athena was also accredited with the various duties women were expected to do and she was portrayed at having great capabilities in each of these duties. This was the reason behind the title of Ergane.

Athena was considered to be the keeper of the law and justice and was thought to have established the antediluvian court of the Areiopagus and would give one vote towards the person accused. The title for this role was axiopoinos.

In her role as a goddess of war, Athena is the opposite to her brother Ares. Instead of being the savage war goddess, she was a cautious war deity. She was the protector of many Greek heroes who sought her for advice during war including Heracles, Achilles and Odysseus. She helped Zeus and Heracles during the Giant War, trapping Enceladus under Sicily and she was the one to kill Pallas. In her character of war goddess, she is typically shown in her armour, complete with Zeus' aegis and he even let her use his thunderbolt. Homer tells that she favours those who treat each battle with caution instead of rushing in head on.

The Orphic Hymns assign her personality to be both male and female and this is why we see in Homer's works that she is called a virgin goddess. She features in one myth where Teiresias was blinded by accidently seeing her naked. However, later writers tell that she was the mother of Apollo by Hephaestus which may have come about when the Ionians exported the cult of Apollo into Attica and placed him into Athena's family. Another son of Athena and Hephaestus was said to be Lychnus.

Apollo

Apollo was one of the Olympian twins born to Zeus and Leto. His grandmother was Phoebe, a first generation Titan. He is diversely recognized as the god of sun and light, prophecy and truth, plague, healing, poetry and music. He was also a recognized patron of Delphi and so was an oracular god.

Homer states that Apollo was one of the great Greek deities and the son of Zeus and Leto, but it is Hesiod who makes Artemis his twin sister. However, neither writer mentions the location where he was born unless we use the title Lukegenes which certain scholars believes it to mean 'Born in Lycia' whereas others see it translate as 'Born in Light'. The legend of his birth was extremely popular and numerous towns and cities state theirs as the place he was born in.

In the Ephesian version, Artemis and Apollo were born in an orchard near Ephesus; both Tegyra and Zoster state the same but for their own – some versions mention Artemis but others do not. In Egypt, Apollo was the result of a union between Dionysus and the Egyptian goddess Isis. But the most popular version of his parentage was that he was the son of Zeus and Leto. When Hera, the wife of Zeus, discovered Leto was pregnant, she had her pursued so that Leto could not rest and give birth. She finally landed on the floating island of Delos and after nine days of labour, Apollo was born under an olive tree (others claim a palm tree). All the other goddesses, apart from Hera and Eileithyia, helped her during this time but the latter goddess offered her services once she knew what was going on.

Until the birth of Apollo, Delos had been floating around the ocean but once the god was born, pillars secured it right to the very centre of the earth. The goddess Themis gave the baby Apollo nectar and ambrosia and once he had sampled the food of the gods, he commanded someone to give him a lyre and a bow, announcing that he would be the one to inform men what Zeus demanded. Delos, excited and happy at last, was covered in a blanket of golden flowers.

Apollo may be one of the great Olympic gods but he is actually portrayed as one who depends on his father, the originator of the powers Apollo wields. In fact, the powers Apollo holds may seem to be different but are, in fact, related to one another and may be just the result of one power.

The titles of hekatos and ekatebolos indicate that he was a deity whose darts never miss a target. It was therefore believed that any sudden deaths were caused by the darts (arrows) of Apollo and it was these arrows that he sent into the Greek camps during the Trojan War. Hyginus claims that when the god was just four days old, he ventured to Mount Parnassus and slew the dragon Python, the same monster that had been sent by Hera to follow Leto. The context of Apollo being called a destroyer of the wicked led to the conception of his name, related to the word 'apollumi' which means to destroy.

Just as Apollo had the power to start plagues and diseases, he had the ability to save men from them. Later writers give him titles such as alexikakos to show him as a benevolent deity. As such, he was called the father of Paceon and Asclepius, both gods of healing.

As a god of prophecy, we see Apollo using this ability numerous times in his myths, and no more apparent than at Delphi. His gift of prophecy was given to him by Zeus and he is therefore called the seer of his father. One of his most famous myths concerns how he took possession of the Oracle at Delphi. The legend says that the oracle was overseen by Themis and was guarded by the monstrous dragon, Python. Apollo managed to kill Python and took control of the oracle.

There are numerous theories as to the origin of Apollo – some scholars place his origins in the north, some in Egypt. But no matter what, Apollo was one of the more influential gods in Greece. However, despite this Apollo wasn't adopted by the Romans when the rest of the Greek gods were assimilated into Roman culture. We know that the Romans visited the Oracle at Delphi early on, even before the Roman kings were expelled, but he wasn't worshiped until around 430 BCE.

Artemis

She was regarded as one of the most respected Olympians. She had a twin sibling, Apollo. They were fathered by Zeus through Leto. She personified the hunt, virginity, wilderness, childbirth and was a formidable guardian of young girls. Artemis is often depicted as a huntress and seen with a bow and arrows. The cypress and deer were extremely sacred to her.

As a child she was thrashed by Hera. In grief she climbed onto her father's lap and asked for six wishes that Zeus promptly agreed to. One of these wishes was that she always wanted to remain a virgin. She gathered her own pack of virgin hunters. She was known to have shown the strongest intimacy with her hunting partner, Orion. Orion was later killed, either by Artemis or by Gaia. Some sources say that the overprotective Apollo was the one who sent the scorpion that killed Orion.

The goddess' name originates from the word artemes, which translates as healthy or vigorous; as such, she was considered to be the deity that was vigorous and gifted that vigour and health upon others. Homer doesn't mention Artemis as the twin sister of Apollo but Hesiod does and both claim her to be a daughter of Zeus and Leto but Pausanias names Demeter as her mother with Leto acting as her nurse. Aeschylus gives her the name Ietogeneia. An Egyptian version calls her a daughter of Dionysus and Isis.

The most popular version of her birth places it on the island of Delos alongside her twin brother; another version claims she was born at Ortygia close to Ephesus, with later writers claiming Crete. Some sources say although she was a sister of Apollo, she was born far earlier than he and was able to help Leto give birth to him.

As Apollo's sister, Artemis was considered the female aspect of her brother. This connection between Apollo and Artemis was often portrayed as the relationship between married couples and, indeed, there are sources which claim that Artemis was, in fact, Apollo's wife. As his female counterpart, Artemis is typically depicted with a bow and arrows and is capable of creating plagues and diseases amongst humans. The sudden deaths amongst women is said to be because Artemis had shot an arrow at them.

Like Apollo, Artemis was also capable of healing and curing maladies amongst humans. In this role she is known as a thea soteira. In the myths concerning Aeneas, she cured him of his injuries when he was brought to her brother's sanctuary. During the Trojan War she was on the side of the Trojans and cared for a man, ensuring that his fields bloomed and lived to a ripe old age.

Another of her roles was that of a protector of children. Here she was given the title paidotrophos and as a protector of young animals, and those dwelling in the forests, she became known as a goddess of the hunt. Artemis was the divine huntress, known as the stag killer.

As with her brother, Artemis was unmarried and remained a virgin (unlike Apollo on this issue). Her priests and priestesses were to stay pure and never indulge in physical acts of love and if they were caught in doing so, they were punished harshly.

Whilst Artemis and Apollo have many similarities between them, there are aspects where they don't correspond. For instance, Artemis has no connection to music, poetry or even foresight. Whereas Apollo had a strong connection to the sun, Artemis was believed to be associated with the moon, although, it should be pointed out that this notion wasn't conceived until a much later date.

Artemis was worshipped throughout Greece and in neighbouring lands. As such, the local equivalents were identified with Artemis. The Artemis worshipped along the coastline of Tauris was honoured with human sacrifices; in Sparta, young boys were tormented in her temples so that the altar was covered in blood, an act established by Lycurgus who replaced the earlier human sacrifices made in her honour.

The task of tracing the initial source of all Artemis' characteristics to a singular notion is simply too difficult to achieve. It is clear that as the goddess was introduced from region to region, characteristics from pre-established cult goddesses were used and incorporated into the new goddess.

Artemis is portrayed in art in various ways depending on what role she plays (as a goddess of the hunt or of the moon). She is depicted as a beautiful young woman in both roles but in the first she is shown with a high forehead, with her hair tied up with some trailing down, wearing or holding a bow and arrow. In the latter, she wears a robe which touches the floor with a veil covering her head and a crescent moon positioned above her whilst she holds a torch.

Ares

The name "Ares" literally translates to battle. He was born to Zeus and Hera. He is a total contrast to the strategist Athena. Unlike Athena, Ares specializes in the pure, untamed and violent aspect of war. Relying primarily on brute strength rather than laying out winning strategies.

His usual companions were his sons, Phobos (Fear) and Deimos (Terror) along with his lover/sister Enyo. These three accompanied him on his war chariot. Ares received some bad publicity when he ended up on the losing side during the battle of Troy. He is also infamously known as the lover of Aphrodite who was married to Hephaestus. This immoral relationship has often been the object of ridicule in the Greek god circles.

Whilst Athena was regarded as the wisdom in battle, Ares was considered the manifestation of brute strength, force and savagery of war. As such, Ares was more of the personification of the horrors of war. Ares took great delight in killing men on the battlefield and ruining entire towns. He was such a lover of the battlefield that he earned the anger of the rest of the gods – and even that of his parents – and this makes him one of the most hated deities in the Greek pantheon. Homer portrays him as a deity of which all the personifications of the aspects of war surrounds him in *The Iliad*, but in *The Odyssey*, Homer has portrayed him a little less frightening.

With his lust for the battlefield, destruction and brute strength, it would be easy to think that the ancient Greeks believed that he was invincible in war. However, this was clearly not the case. Indeed, in many myths, when Ares was confronted by Zeus and even other divinities, he was subdued. Diomedes was able to injure him when aided by Athena, causing him to cry out so loud that it sounded like 10,000 warriors screaming out in unison. Athena was able to bring him down by throwing a boulder at him during a human war.

If this wasn't enough, the giant Aloadae was able to capture and chain him, making the god of war his captive for 13 months until Hermes was able to free him. When Typhon attempted to conquer Olympus, Ares fled to Egypt (as with the other gods) in the form of a fish. Even Heracles was able to beat him in one myth. Despite the numerous times he was defeated, the god of war was triumphant in many other cases.

Ares features in a number of myths, including the affair he had with Aphrodite in which the lovers were caught in a net fashioned by her husband Hephaestus and were shamed before all the gods; the slaying of Adonis, the human lover of Aphrodite whom he was incredibly jealous of; the metamorphosis of Cadmus and his bride into serpents; and the slaying of Poseidon's son Halirrhotius who had tried to rape Ares' daughter, Alcippe, but was acquitted in the Olympian court.

The ancient Greeks saw the Thracian tribes as a warlike people and so it led to the belief that Ares resided there. In Scythia, one of his major cult centres, Ares was honoured in the shape of a sword and was offered sacrifices of horses, cattle and men.

Ares was also honoured in Colchis (modern day Georgia), the city where King Aeetes had possession of the Golden Fleece. The fleece was hid in a tree in a grove which was holy to the god. The island known as Arestias near Colchis, was home to the Stymphalian birds and a sacred place to him.

Ares was not a popular god in regards to ancient Greek worship. There were temples dedicated to him in Laconia, Athens, Olympia and Sparta, the latter place conducting human sacrifices in his name, but temples were typically erected outside the city walls, most likely in the belief that he would stop any enemies coming too near the city.

Scholars believe that the worship of Ares was introduced into Greece from the north, most likely originating from Thrace. The earliest representations of Ares are from Alcamenes, who gives us the model of the god. Indeed, the majority of depictions of this war-like deity come from coins and gemstones.

Aphrodite

As is common in Greek literature there is more than one story behind her birth. One states that she rose from the sea foam that was produced when Cronus cut off Uranus' genitals and threw them into the sea. Other sources cite that she was born to Zeus and Dione, whereas later writers state she was the daughter of Cronus and Euonyme or that of Uranus and Hemera.

Aphrodite was extremely beautiful and was regarded the goddess of beauty, love, procreation and pleasure. Such was her beauty that the Olympians feared that they might fall out due to rivalry over her. As a solution, Zeus married her off to Hephaestus. He was deformed and ugly, so he wasn't considered to be a formidable threat. She had many lovers out of wedlock spanning across god and men alike.

Hesiod and the Homeric Hymn to Aphrodite both claim that after she materialised out of the sea and onto the shores of Cythera she then ventured to Cyprus. Whilst she was walking along the coast, flowers grew where her footsteps fell and Eros and Himeros escorted her to the heavens where she was admired for her beauty and the male deities desired her for their bride.

At her very basic and original level, Aphrodite was the personification of the procreative natural force, the mother of the human race. This can be traced back to her role in the myth where Typhon battles with the gods for control of Olympus; here, Aphrodite transforms herself into a fish, a creature which was seen to have the most reproductive power. However, the ancient Greeks saw her as a goddess of love, who stirred men's hearts and through this, controlled all living beings.

In mythology, Aphrodite had two sides to her nature – on one side, she was loving and caring to those who honoured her, bestowing blessings and protecting them in times of danger. On the other hand, she could be cruel and unforgiving to those who angered her. In terms of beauty and grace, Aphrodite clearly won against the other goddesses and she was attended by the Charites, the Horae and other minor deities connected to both these ideals. Due to her sea birth, Aphrodite was believed to have some degree of control over the sea according to later writers.

As Paris, the prince of Troy, had declared Aphrodite as the fairest goddess, she sided with the Trojans. She protected several Trojans, including Paris from Menelaus but was wounded by Diomedes when she tried to rescue her son, Aeneas, from the battle. When she returned to Olympus and complained to Dione about the situation, both Hera and Athena made a mockery of her. In *The Iliad*, she protects the body of Prince Hector and massaged ambrosia onto it.

Popular myths tell that Aphrodite was married to the lame smith-god, Hephaestus, but in *The Iliad* she was the wife of Charis. She was said to have engaged in an affair with the war god, Ares, but was caught in a net fashioned by her husband. Afterwards, she and Ares had several children together, including Harmonia, Deimos and Phobos.

Aphrodite had relationships with several other deities and even mortals. By Dionysus she was the mother of Priapus and Bacchus; by Hermes she gave birth to Hermaphroditus; and Rhodos and Herophilus by Poseidon. By the mortal man Anchises, she became the mother of Aneas and Lyrus.

Aphrodite had major cult centres in several places in Greece, including Cyprus and Cythera. One of her most ancient cult centres was located at Mount Ida as well as being worshipped in Sparta, Athens, Corinth and Sicily. She was most likely imported from Syria initially to Cyprus, and then introduced to the rest of Greece. However, although her personality is most certainly from Mesopotamia, her legends and aspects of her worship are entirely Greek in nature so it is likely that she was imported in very early times.

Hephaestus

Hephaestus was born to Zeus and Hera. He was the god of the smithy and so was associated with craftsmen, blacksmiths, artisans, sculptors, fire, volcanoes and metals. Due to his expertise in metal manipulation he crafted the weapons of all the gods in Olympus. A hammer, a pair of tongs and an anvil were his favorite symbols. He created all the thrones for the gods.

Most of the known and famous weapons were his creations. He even made automatons to help him in his work. He was rejected by Hera at birth because he was born lame. He took revenge by designing a throne for Hera that would not let her stand up once she sat on it. He refused to let her out of her predicament even though the gods begged him. He was exiled from Olympus and sent to earth. Finally, Dionysus brought an intoxicated Hephaestus back to Olympus and released his mother from her throne. He was the only god to return to Olympus after being exiled.

The most common version of Hephaestus' birth was a later account, where Hera conceived him without any help from Zeus, as she was jealous that Zeus had given birth to his daughter Athena on his own by having his head spilt open. However, another popular story was that Hephaestus had spilt the head of Zeus open to free Athena so in that case, Hephaestus was older than Athena.

Another version of his birth states that the god was born from the thigh of Hera and wasn't told who his father was for quite some time. Furious at the deception, he fashioned the throne that captured Hera. He only released her when she finally admitted that she and Zeus were his parents.

Hephaestus was the representation of the power of fire. This was both in its natural elements such as volcanoes, but also the fire which was used to create art and objects. From the moment of his birth, Hephaestus was seen to be weak and hated by his mother, so was thrown out of Olympus. After falling for an entire day and night, the god landed in the ocean and was raised for nine years by Thetis and Eurynome. In exchange, he created beautiful ornaments and trinkets for them.

On Olympus, Hephaestus dwelled in his own palace which was said to have shone as brilliantly as the stars. Inside the palace was his workshop, where he made exquisite items for both humans and his fellow gods. He was said to have created many items, including the giant bronze man, Talos, who guarded the island of Crete. In later accounts, the writers transport his workshop from his Olympian home and into the depths of a volcanic island.

Hephaestus was married to Charis in *The Iliad*, in *The Odyssey* his wife was Aphrodite and then Aglaia by Hesiod in his Theogony. Homer doesn't say that Hephaestus had any offspring in his works, but the god was accredited as the father of many by later writers. In *The Iliad*, Hephaestus was a Greek supporter but the Trojans paid him homage and he even rescued a Trojan from being slain by Diomedes.

Hephaestus was considered to be an inferior counterpart to that of Athena; they both practiced the arts and taught humans certain arts to improve their lives. Despite the amount of knowledge he imparted on Greek society, however, he was still regarded as inferior to the goddess.

In art, Hephaestus was typically depicted as a strong, muscular bearded man, usually holding a tool of some kind, wearing a cap and chiton, allowing his right shoulder and arm to be bare.

Hermes

Hermes was born to Zeus and Maia. He is the second youngest in the line of the Olympians. He was regarded as the patron of boundaries. He was known to be very quick, shrewd and cunning. He moved between the mortal and divine worlds seamlessly. He donned the role of being a messenger and emissary to the gods and men alike. He is known to shelter travelers, herdsmen and thieves. A caduceus is his symbol of power. It is a winged staff around which two snakes are wrapped.

Hermes features in a number of legends. When he was just a couple of hours old, he escaped from his crib and ventured to Pieiria and stole the oxen of Apollo. In *The Iliad* and *The Odyssey*, Homer does not retell this story, but he does highlight Hermes' character as a sneaky thief. Other accounts of this myth place it when Hermes was much older and he dons a pair of sandals and escorted the stolen cattle to Pylos where he slays two of the beasts and hides the others in a cave. The hides of the animals were fastened to a boulder, and a section of the meat was consumed and the rest was offered as a sacrifice to the Olympic gods. As such, Hermes is considered to be the originator of sacrifices to the gods. After this, he journeyed back to Cyllene. Here, he found a tortoise outside his cave. He positioned several strings across the shell and therefore created the lyre.

Whilst this was going on, Apollo, discovering the culprit through his gift of foresight, travelled to Cyllene and accused him in front of Maia. The goddess didn't believe him and showed Apollo her baby still in his cradle, but Apollo took the infant to Zeus and demanded that his oxen be returned. Hermes declared that he hadn't taken Apollo's herd but when he realised no one believed him, he took him to Pylos where his oxen were still hidden away. However, when Apollo heard the music Hermes played on his lyre, he permitted him to keep the herd.

The central theme in the myths and legends of Hermes show him as a herald of the gods and this is portrayed in the epic works penned by Homer. He was almost certainly an ancient god worshipped by the Pelasgians or from prehistoric Arcadia, a nature god, but as he was assimilated into the Greek pantheon, he lost that original aspect to his personality. In sacrifices, Hermes was offered animal tongues, illustrating the belief that he was skilled in speech.

In addition to this, Hermes was considered to be the god of caution when it came to social get-togethers. With his gift of cunning, these aspects made his a god of thieves and stealing, but the way he carried out these schemes had a particular elegance to them.

Hermes played an important part as a god of the underworld. In his role as a psuchopompos, he escorted the souls of the recently dead down to the underworld where they would be ferried over the River Styx.

Hermes was worshipped throughout Greece and neighbouring lands but his major cult centre was in Arcadia. Here, the legend states that Lycaon erected the first sanctuary in his name. From Arcadia, he was exported to Athens and then all throughout the country. Festivals in his honour were known as Hermaia.

In art, Hermes was portrayed as a young bearded man holding a staff and wearing a travelling hat to which wings were fastened upon (this was only seen in later works). There are numerous depictions showing him with winged sandals but Homer does not mention these. His staff was originally plain, then two ribbons were incorporated into the design before they were later changed to snakes.

Hestia

She was considered as the goddess of the hearth and family. Unlike her siblings, she did not choose an emblem for herself. She was entitled to the first offering at every sacrifice in a household. Her position as the twelfth Olympian is highly speculated. Some say she gave way for Dionysus so as to maintain stability on Mount Olympus. She did not have any consorts. She was not survived by any children either.

Hestia was the eldest daughter of Cronus and Rhea, the first of his children that be swallowed. She was initially regarded as one of the 12 great Olympic gods and was desired by both Apollo and Poseidon but she made an oath to remain a virgin.

The relationship between Hestia and her brother and nephew, which can be seen in this myth, can also be seen in Delphi, where she was worshipped with both gods at the temple of Delphi. She also appears with Poseidon in Olympia where both siblings are honoured side by side.

Hestia was regarded as the personification of the hearth or, more specifically, the fire of the hearth. The hearth was the centre of the ancient Greek home, and as such, Hestia was seen to be the goddess of the home and all domestic joy and miracles, living at the centre of all Greek homes. Due to this, she is frequently shown with Hermes. The hearth was the place where sacrifices were made and so she inherits the role of guardian of sacrifices, sharing a portion of all sacrifices made to the gods. This is why, when sacrifices were made, Hestia was called upon first to receive a section of the sacrifice before the rest was offered to other deities.

When people took important oaths, they would call upon Hestia and it was by the home hearth that the applicant would ask for help from the occupants of the house. The town hearth became the sacred symbol of the town as one great big home, and it was here at this sacred communal hearth that sacrifices were made to her. Guests from foreign lands would be received here and when settlers from the town moved to colonise a different region, they would take the fire from the public hearth to light the hearth in the new town.

There were only a limited number of temples erected in Hestia's name in Greece but in reality, every town hearth was the place of her worship.

Dionysus

Dionysus was considered to be the god of ecstasy, celebrations and wine. In short, he was the party god. He is the only Olympian god to have a mortal parent. He was fathered by Zeus through the mortal Theban princess, Semele. He is also the youngest Olympian. His most popular symbols were grapevines and leopards. He was married to Ariadne.

Dionysus, whose name means 'Twice Born', was the 13th Olympic god and was said to have been given his seat by Hestia who stepped down from her position so that he could have it. The most popular version of his birth is as follows: Semele, a beautiful princess, the daughter of King Cadmus, became pregnant by Zeus. Hera, the jealous wife of Zeus, went to Semele in the form of an old woman and told her to ask her lover to reveal his true shape. When Zeus next visited her, she begged him to show her his true shape and despite all his ways to convince her otherwise, in the end he relented and appeared before her as thunder and lightning. Scared, Semele gave birth to a baby boy far too early and so Zeus cut open his thigh and placed the infant in it until he was ready to be born again, hence the name 'twice born'.

As there were several ancient versions of this myth, scholars believe that there were more than one god that were eventually assimilated together to create a singular deity and given the name Dionysus.

When Dionysus was born for the second time, Zeus was said to have given him to Hermes, Persephone or Rhea and asked Ino to raise the boy as a girl. Hera, still enraged, drove Ino to madness and so Zeus transformed his son into a ram and gave him to the nymphs of Mount Nysa to be raised. When the boy was grown up, the nymphs were positioned amongst the stars.

Dionysus' origins appear to be as a manifestation of the intoxication of nature, allowing man to be free of sobriety for a time. The first time we see Dionysus as a god of wine is in Thrace and then it was exported south to Helicon, then onto Thebes, Naxos and then throughout Greece. Worship was carried to Sicily, Italy and even Egypt.

Hecate

Hecate was an important and interesting goddess in Greek mythology. It seems that she existed among the Carians of Anatolia long before the Greek gods cemented their place and so had to be brought into the fold. This is why there are several origin stories for her.

Hesiod's Theogony states that she was the daughter of Perses and Asteria. If you remember, Asteria was the sister of Leto who gave birth to Apollo and Artemis. All together, Selene, Artemis and Hecate are known as the moon goddesses and are often confused with each other.

Other accounts of her birth state that she was a Titan who helped Zeus in his war against the Titans and for this Zeus rewarded her greatly. Whatever be her origin, it is clear that she was a very important goddess and had the favour of Zeus. She is often shown residing on the hand of Zeus.

Over the years she became the goddess of the moon, crossroads, entrance-ways, dogs, light, magic, witchcraft, herbs, ghosts, necromancy and sorcery. She is said to have had rule over all three domains of earth, sea and sky. She is depicted sometimes in a triple form, either having three bodies or having three heads on one body. She's depicted holding, fire, a key, serpents, dagger and several other items.

She is said to have empathized with Demeter when she lost Persephone and she was the one who told her to ask Helios, the sun god. Later she also accompanied Persephone during her annual visits from the underworld. She never got married or had any kids. She also held power over storms which made her a revered goddess for sailors as well.

Hecate is highly revered in Greek society and is said to have great powers to bestow on those who please her. She helps men win wars and games alike. She can make the flock of sheep increase in number and provide good fleece.

Dogs are known to be her guardians and companions. Apart from dogs she is also said to favour other animals like the pole cat, the red mullet fish, the frog, cow, boar, serpent and horse. She is also associated with several plants as she is known as the goddess of the knowledge of herbs and poisonous plants. The Yew was sacred to her and she also was associated with the oak. Garlic was associated with her cult and the cypress tree was also a symbol for her. Other poisonous, medicinal and psychoactive plants are also associated with her including aconite, belladonna, dittany and mandrake.

The Deipnon was a festival that celebrated Hecate on the moonless night of every lunar month. Food was offered to Hecate in order to placate the dead souls that were not at rest.

Pan

Pan was a very old and important god. He existed in different cultures long before Greek mythology took its shape. Subsequently he was included into Greek mythology. What's interesting about Pan is that he represented the pagan religions and the rise of Christianity started when the pagan religions were subdued and it was said that the great Pan was dead. Some scholars say that Pan had to die so that Jesus could live. This statement shows the importance of Pan in the religions of that time.

In Greek mythology, Pan is the god of the wild, the shepherds, rustic music, flocks of sheep and goats, and nature of the wild mountains. He was also considered to be the god of fields, groves, glens and fertility of spring. The Greeks also thought of him as the god of theatrical criticism and that's why today we have the verb pan which means to severely criticize a show, as in "the critics panned the show."

Pan is shown as a bearded man with goat legs and hind quarters. He also has little goat horns. He plays a reed based wind instrument. He is often depicted with a phallus as he was famous for his sexual powers. He was always lusting after one or the other nymph who were always rejecting him or trying to escape him. His most famous conquest is the moon goddess Selene who he seduced by wrapping himself in sheep skin to hide his goat hairs.

His origin is not easy to understand in Greek mythology. This is because he existed long before Greek mythology itself. Some say that he was the son of Hermes, others say Zeus or even Dionysus. Apollo is also sometimes thought of as his father. Since he existed before the Olympians, some sources say that he was the son of Cronus. Sources are also not clear if there was just one Pan or more.

Aegipan was supposed to be the son of Pan by some sources while in other traditions he was the father of Pan. Aegipan was raised by Amalthea, the same goat that raised Zeus. Later during the war against the Titans, Aegipan helped his foster brother by letting out a horrible scream that scattered the Titans. This is why the word panic comes from Pan. It was a fear induced in anyone who heard him scream. When Gaia sent Typhon to destroy Zeus, Aegipan and Hermes found Zeus' "sinews" that Typhon had hidden and helped him defeat Typhon.

Pan began to be worshipped in Arcadia, where the mountainous people had a different culture than rest of Greece. Pan wasn't worshipped in temples and instead out in the open or in caves. Only two temples were ever built for Pan, one in Neda River gorge in Peloponnese and one in Apollonopolis Magna in Egypt.

The myths related to Pan are numerous and often about his sexual exploits. His reed flute came when he chased a water nymph called Syrinx. She hid herself along with her sisters in the form of reeds. Since Pan didn't know which reed she was, he plucked several of them and cut them up in varying lengths and tied them up to form his flute.

Another one of his myths is that he once challenged Apollo to a musical competition. Tmolus, a mountain god, was chosen as the judge. Apollo easily won but Pan's supporter Midas felt that the judgement was wrong. Apollo turned his ears into that of a donkey's because he couldn't tell the difference between their music.

Other Minor Deities
Triton
Triton was the son of Poseidon and his wife Amphitrite. He was half human and half fish, having a lower body of a fish. This is probably where the myth of the merman comes from. He carried a trident like his father but also had a conch shell that he could blow to calm a raging sea or bring forth a storm on a calm sea. Triton had a

daughter named Pallas and also fostered Athena for a while. Pallas was accidentally killed by Athena while the two goddesses were sparring.

Triton is also said to have created the race of Tritons; mermaids and mermen who are gods and goddesses of the sea. Tritons are often seen escorting marine deities. A myth tells that when Misenus, the son of Aeolus, challenged the gods, Triton killed him by drowning him in the sea. Triton is supposed to reside in the waters off Aegae. Sometimes he is said to live with his parents Poseidon and Amphitrite in the golden palace at the bottom of the sea.

Nereus

Nereus was the Old Man of the Sea. He was the son of Pontus and Gaia. As such he was from the time of the Titans. Later he was replaced by Triton in Greek mythology. He was a shape shifter and could take shapes of monsters. Sometimes he was shown as an old man with the lower body of a fish, holding a staff.

He was known to be rightful and just. He never told lies and was gentle and trustworthy. He never forgot what was right and what was wrong. He married Doris and fathered the Nereids and Nerites who was a consort of Aphrodite.

Proteus

Proteus was the other, old man of the sea. The confusion between Proteus and Nereus could be because of different names given to the same god during different times. Proteus was said to be the son of Poseidon so he could be the Olympian version of Nereus. Like Nereus he too could change his shape. He had the ability to foretell the future and answer questions about the past but he would only do it when someone was able to catch him.

Menelaus caught him to find out about which gods he had angered and how to propitiate them. Proteus told him many things including that Agamemnon had been murdered and Odysseus was stranded on an island. Proteus comes from the word protos which translates to "first". This makes sense as Proteus was the first son of Poseidon.

Hebe

Hebe was the goddess of youth, the wife of Heracles and the daughter of Zeus and Hera. Hebe means "youth" or "prime of life". She was the cupbearer for the Olympians and helped the gods in other ways; like drawing baths for Ares or helping Hera mount her chariot. She is shown in classical depictions as wearing a sleeveless dress, holding a cup and with Zeus in the form of an eagle, drinking from the cup.

She married Heracles and had two children; Alexiares and Anicetus. She was also known as the goddess of forgiveness and pardons. In Sicyon, the Phliasians pardoned suppliants to worship Hebe who they also called Dia.

Iris

Iris was the messenger of the gods and a personification of the rainbow. She could travel with the speed of the wind between all the realms, including Olympus, earth, the underworld and the depths of the sea. She was the daughter of Thaumas and Electra, a cloud nymph. She had four sisters; Arke, Aello, Celaeno and Ocypete. She is depicted as a rainbow or as a young woman with wings on her shoulders. She is associated with communication, messages, new endeavours and the rainbow.

Hermes was also the messenger of the gods and the two are sometimes interchanged in myths. She too carried a winged staff like Hermes. She is also known with several epithets such as Chrysopteron (golden winged), Podas Okea (swift footed), Podenemos okea (wind-swift foot), Roscida (dewy) and Thaumantias (daughter of Thaumas).

Nike
Nike was the winged goddess of victory. She was the daughter of the Titan Pallas and the goddess Styx. Her siblings included Kratos (strength), Bia (force) and Zelus (zeal). She is shown as a winged woman in most portrayals.

The myth goes that Styx brought all of her children to aid Zeus during his war against the Titans. Nike became the charioteer of Zeus and flew around the battlefield to award glory to the victors. She was close to Athena and is said to have been standing on the hand of Athena in her statue located in the Pantheon.

Horae
The Horae were the goddesses of the seasons. They were either represented as the personification of the seasons, or the hours of the day, or as the personification of natural order and justice. There is a lot of confusion as how many Horae there were and what their names were. But most of them are thought to be the daughters of Zeus and Themis. They were said to be the gatekeepers of Olympus.

The first trio of Horae is associated with the seasons. They are: Thallo (spring), Auxo (summer) and Carpo (autumn). The second trio is related to law and order. These are: Dike (justice), Eunomia (order) and Eirene (peace). One source puts forward a third trio: Pherusa (substance), Euporie (abundance) and Orthosie (prosperity).

Sometimes all of these nine goddesses were taken together and considered the 9 Horae, representing the 9 hours of the day. There was another, less popular list of 12 Horae that also represented the 12 hours of the day. These were: Auge (first light), Anatolia (sunrise), Musica (morning hour of music and study), Gymnasia (morning hour of exercise), Nympha (morning hour for bathing/washing), Mesembria (noon), Sponde (libations poured after lunch), Elete (prayer, the first afternoon work hour), Acte (eating and pleasure, second afternoon work hour), Hesperis (end of afternoon and beginning of evening), Dysis (sunset), Arctus (night sky).

Moirae
The Moirae were also known as the Fates and like the Furies, predated the Olympians. They might have begun with just one Moira but later became fixed at three: Clotho (spinner), Lachesis (allotter) and Atropos (unturnable). They originate

from cultures that predated the Greeks and similar concepts are found in Egyptian, Vedic and Avestan cultures.

They were said to be the daughters of Ananke (destiny or necessity). Later they were called the daughters of Zeus and Themis. Their relationship with Zeus is also argued about. Some say that they ruled over all the gods and not even Zeus could control them. But later Zeus was shown as the only one who could control them but even then he wasn't shown as able to change anyone's fate.

The Moirae are shown as three old women, sometimes crippled and ugly. They are severe, inflexible and stern. Clotho spins the life of thread at the birth of each man. Lachesis measures the thread with her scale and decides how much life each man gets. Atropos then cuts the life of thread and decides the death of the new born child. Once decided, nothing can then change his fate.

Charites
The Charites were another trio of Greek mythology and they were also known as the Graces. They were the goddesses of charm, beauty, creativity, fertility, nature, celebration, festivities and amusement. There most common names are Aglaea (splendour), Euphrosyne (mirth) and Thalia (good cheer).

Usually they are thought to be the daughters of Zeus and Eurynome but at other times their parents have also been said to be Dionysus and Aphrodite or Helios and Aegle. They are often seen together with Aphrodite. The Cephissus River near Delphi was sacred to them.

Sometimes other names are associated with the Charites and their number can also vary. Some of these names are: Auxo (growth), Hegemone (queen), Peitho (persuasion), Antheia (blossoms), Eudaimonia (happiness), Paidia (play), Pandaisia (banquet) and Pannychis (night festivities) etc.

Muses
The Muses were the daughters of Zeus and Mnemosyne. As mentioned in the section on Mnemosyne in chapter 1 of this book, their names were Calliope (epic poetry), Clio (history), Euterpe (lyric poetry), Thalia (comedy), Melpomene (tragedy), Terpsichore (dance), Erato (love poetry), Polyhymnia (sacred poetry) and Urania (astronomy).

They are the goddesses of inspiration in the fields of art, literature, science, drama, poetry etc. Originally the Muses might have been three and later on increased to nine. In the earlier versions the three Muses weren't given specific fields of art as given to the nine later on. Since knowledge was passed on in the form of songs and poetry before scrolls or books were used, the Muses played an important role in the society. Temples of the Muses were places of education and storage of knowledge. Today the Museum can still be said to be a temple to the Muses. The word Music also finds it origins in the Muses.

These are the major and minor gods of Greek mythology. We've covered most of the famous ones that were popular all over Greece. There were some minor deities that were worshiped only in one city or a particular region that might not have been mentioned here but we've covered all of the popular ones. In the next chapter we'll talk about some more myths related to Greek gods.

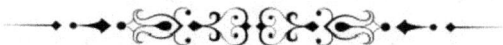

Chapter 3

The Myths of the Gods

The Myths of the Gods

Mount Olympus

Mount Olympus is sometimes thought to have been the real mountain in Greece with the same name. But some believe that the residence of the gods was a mystical mountain, not a part of earth. It wasn't heaven either but a different place common to all the Olympians. It had a great gate made up of clouds behind which the gods lived and feasted on ambrosia and nectar. They listened to Apollo's lyre and enjoyed perfect peace and sunshine. Rain, snow and bad weather were absent from Mount Olympus and the view in all directions was of open sky and clouds far below the mountain.

Helios and Phaeton

Helios was one of the three children of Hyperion and Theia and was the personification of the sun. He is represented as riding the chariot of the sun across the sky. Four fiery steeds drive the chariot. Helios and the counterpart Olympian, Apollo, are often mixed up as they both represent the light.

One famous myth related to Helios is that his son Phaeton asked to drive the chariot one day and he tried to explain to him that the chariot is not easy to drive and the horses are fiery and difficult to control. He said that even Zeus doesn't dare drive his chariot but his son insisted and in the end Helios agreed to let him drive his chariot. But Phaeton lost control and the chariot went too close to earth. It dried up the oceans and rivers and burned the vegetation, creating the Sahara desert. The entire earth would have been burnt so Zeus had to interfere and kill Phaeton with his thunderbolt. Phaeton fell like a falling star into the river Eridanos.

Helios had a lot of children with different wives. He had a strong cult in ancient times but with the end of the Dark Ages his cult waned in favor of the other gods. He was relegated to a minor god and was worshipped in a few places like the island of Rhodes.

Selene and Endymion

Selene was the goddess of the moon and along with Eos and Helios she formed the three children of the Titans Hyperion and Theia. Just like Helios, she drove her moon chariot across the sky every night. Just like Helios was often confused with Apollo, Selene was confused with Artemis. Selene, Artemis and Hecate are known as the lunar goddesses.

A myth about Selene says that she fell in love with the mortal Endymion and came down every night from the sky to steal kisses while he slept. Endymion was in an eternal sleep and there are different accounts as to how he ended up this way. Some accounts say that he was the grandson of Zeus and had received the power to put himself into an eternal sleep so that he remained ageless and deathless. One account says that Selene herself put him in an eternal sleep so that she could have him forever.

The Birth of Apollo and Artemis

Leto was most famous for being the mother of Apollo and Artemis. Zeus made her pregnant which incurred the wrath of Zeus' wife Hera. Hera banned Leto from giving birth on land and had her chased by monsters from the underworld. Leto managed to find a floating island called Delos which was not connected to the seabed and so technically wasn't "land". After the birth of Apollo, Zeus attached the island to the seabed and the island became sacred to Apollo.

Hera also kidnapped, Eileithyia, the goddess of childbirth, to prevent Leto from giving birth. The other gods tricked Hera into letting her go by distracting her with a necklace made of amber. Leto first gave birth to Artemis, who then helped as midwife for the birth of Apollo. Leto was worshipped as the mother goddess in Lycia and a few other places but in Athens she was relegated to be just the mother of Apollo. After his birth, Apollo killed the monsters that had hounded his mother and tried to prevent his birth.

The Rape of Persephone

Persephone was the daughter of Zeus and Demeter. Zeus had promised Hades that he could have Persephone as his wife but did not tell Demeter about his promise to Hades and the Lord of the Underworld split open the earth and grabbed the young spring goddess (who was picking flowers in the meadow) and took her back down in to the bowels of the earth. Demeter immediately started searching for her daughter.

There are several locations claiming to be the spot where Persephone was abducted from; some sources say it was Enna in Sicily, which highlights its ancient roots. The worship of Demeter was most likely imported to Sicily by settlers from Corinth. Homer states the location is in Nysa in Asia Minor (the abduction of Persephone is not mentioned in *The Iliad* and *The Odyssey*); other sources state Eleusis, an island near Spain called Coonus, Hermione or Pisa.

For 9 days, Demeter searched the world without stopping to eat, sleep or bathe. She came to the goddess Hecate on the 10th day who informed her that she had heard Persephone's cries but had no idea who took her. They journeyed to the sun god Helios who confirmed that he had seen Hades, with the permission of Zeus, snatch Persephone and take her to the Underworld to be his queen. Furious at this, Demeter returned to the Earth and refused to step back on Olympus. Miserable, she caused famine in the land, and would bestow blessings on those who welcomed her and reprimanded those who rejected her. Mankind started to suffer when the fields didn't bear any fruit and seeing this Zeus sent the goddess Iris to Demeter and asked her to return.

Zeus had all the gods try to entice Demeter back to Olympus with extravagant presents but the goddess swore she would not return until she had seen Persephone once more. Zeus sent Hermes down to the Underworld to fetch Persephone but Hades had gave her a pomegranate seed to eat before she left. Once someone had eaten in the underworld, they became a part of it and thus she had to spend three months of the year with Hades and the remainder with her mother; to this Demeter finally relented. It was this myth which explained why no crops grew during winter.

The legend of Demeter and Persephone symbolises the notion that the fruitful powers of nature are hidden during the winter period – Persephone is the ruler in the underworld but is mournful and strives to return to the sunlight (during spring).

Persephone along with Demeter and Hecate are goddesses that existed before the Greek mythological period and were later incorporated into it. Persephone especially had a strong cult even during the Neolithic age as the goddess of agrarian societies of that time. During that time she was known to bear a new god every year that was depicted as a young boy and who would be her consort but then would die and return to the underworld, only to be born again in the next New Year.

Being an old goddess means that there are many names for her. Also because she was the queen of the underworld, Greeks gave her many epithets because, like Hades, they didn't want to utter her real name. Some of these names were Despoina (the mistress), Hagne (pure), Melinoia (honey), Aristi Cthonia (the best chthonic), Kore (the maiden), Neotera (the younger) etc.

Demeter and Persephone together were the prime goddesses of the Eleusinian mysteries and were collectively called The Great Goddesses, The Mistresses or Demeters. Persephone is shown mostly as part of the Rape of Persephone, a scene depicting Hades kidnapping Persephone on his chariot driven by four black horses. As a vegetation goddess she is shown as appearing in the sky above girls dancing in the midst of blooming flowers. In another version she is shown coming out of the ground but without hands or legs and is surrounded by serpents, which makes her look like a vegetable and girls dance around her.

Thesmophoria was a festival celebrated in Athens and later spread to other parts of Greece. This was a women only festival of secret rituals held during autumn to mark the abduction of Persephone by Hades. Sacrifices were also made by burying things in the earth.

The Eleusinian mysteries was a festival celebrated in Eleusis during the autumn sowing as well. This festival celebrated the goddesses, Demeter and Persephone, as well as the agricultural god Triptolemus.

Eos and Cephalus
Eos was the goddess of dawn. Like her siblings Helios and Selene, she also had a chariot in which she traveled across the sky to open the gates of heaven to let the sun come up in the morning. The morning dew was thought to be her tears.

She fell in love with Ares, the god of war and to punish her Aphrodite cursed her to feel insatiable love and sexual desire. Because of this she ended up having several lovers. The most famous myth is her kidnapping of Cephalus with whom she had three sons. Cephalus was already married and kept pining for his wife Procris. Eos let him go but put a curse on the couple because of which Cephalus ended up killing his own wife when he mistook her for an animal he was hunting.

Hypnos and Zeus
Hypnos was the son of Erebus, the primordial god of darkness, son of Chaos, and the goddess of the night, Nyx, daughter of Chaos. As the son of primordial gods, he is older even than the Titans.

He was the god of sleep. His brother was Thanatos, the god of death. He was married to Pasithea who became the deity of hallucination and relaxation. He had three sons known as the Oneiroi; Morpheus, the winged god of dreams, Phobetor the god of nightmares, and Phantasos, the god of illusions and fake dreams.

The most famous myths revolving Hypnos are about the times when he put Zeus to sleep on the command of Hera. The first time it was when Heracles sacked Troy and Hera wanted to punish him. Hypnos put Zeus to sleep and Hera blew angry winds to bring storms in the sea while Heracles sailed back home. When Zeus woke up he was furious and wanted to punish Hypnos but couldn't find him because he hid with his mother Nyx and Zeus was afraid of her.

The second time Hera planned to seduce Zeus and used Hypnos to put him to sleep so that the Danaans could win the Trojan War. Hypnos was reluctant but agreed when Hera promised to marry him to Pasithea. Hera seduced Zeus and Hypnos put him to sleep and then informed Poseidon that he could help the Danaans as Zeus was sleeping. Zeus never found out about him being tricked by Hypnos for a second time, and the Trojans lost.

Erinyes and Orestes

The Erinyes were also known as the Furies and were infernal goddesses of the underworld. Their job was to punish people who did something wrong. They were also known as Harpies and Dirae. Their origin is much older than that of the Olympians. One myth says that they were born when Cronus castrated his father Uranus and his blood fell on earth and they were born out of it. Another myth puts them even before in the timeline as daughters of Nyx, the primordial goddess of the night. But later they were considered daughters of Zeus and Themis.

The number of the Erinyes has mostly been considered to be three and their most common names are Alecto (unceasing), Megaera (grudging) and Tisiphone (vengeful destruction). They live in Erebus (hell) and their job is to punish anyone who breaks an oath or shows disrespect to the natural order such as children disrespecting parents, hosts disrespecting guests etc. They are represented as black maidens with bat wings and red eyes and sometimes with snakes for hair or having a dog's head instead.

A very popular myth about the Erinyes is when Orestes, the son of Agamemnon killed his own mother Clytemnestra to avenge the murder of his father. The Erinyes hounded him but he had only done so on the order of Apollo. Apollo suggested him to seek justice from Athena who set up a court with the citizens of Athens as the jury. The Erinyes formed the prosecution and Apollo the defence. In the end the jury was split down the middle and Athena used her deciding vote to acquit Orestes. The Erinyes were not happy and wanted vengeance but Athena convinced them that they should be the goddesses of justice rather than vengeance. She convinced them by ensuring that they'll receive the worship of the Athenians and also by hinting about the fact that she had access to Zeus' thunderbolt with whom he had destroyed many older gods before. Since then the furies were referred to as the Semnai or venerable ones.

Zephyr and Hyacinth

Zephyrus was one of the Anemoi who were the wind gods. They represented the winds that blew from different directions. They were the sons of Astraeus and Eos, the goddess of dawn. They are represented sometimes as gusts of winds and sometimes in human form with wings. Sometimes they are also represented as horses kept in the stables of Aeolus, the god of storms.

Boreas was the north wind god. He brought winter and was considered strong and bad tempered. He was represented as an old winged man with a beard and hair spiked and frozen, holding a conch shell. Notos was the south wind god who brought storms in late summer and autumn. Eurus was the east wind god but wasn't related to any particular season. He brought warmth and rain. Four other minor wind gods were Kaikias (northeast wind), Apeliotes (southeast wind), Skiron (northwest wind) and Lips (southwest wind).

Zephyrus was the gentle west wind god. He came during the spring and early summer and resulted in the fruiting and flowering of plants. He was said to be the husband of Iris, the goddess of the rainbow. He also abducted the goddess Chloris and made her the goddess of the flowers. With Chloris he fathered a son, Karpos (fruit). He was also the father of Balius and Xanthus, the two horses of Achilles.

The most famous myth related to Zephyrus or Zephyr is that he fell in love with a handsome young Spartan prince, Hyacinth. Apollo was also in love with him. Hyacinth chose Apollo and this drove Zephyr mad with jealousy. While Apollo and Hyacinth played discus, Zephyr made a strong wind blow which caused the discus to hit Hyacinth in the head and killed him. Apollo created the flower Hyacinth from the boy's blood. Apollo was also mad at Zephyr and wanted to punish him but Eros saved him, saying that the deed was done out of love.

With this we've covered most of the myths of the gods of Greek mythology. From the next chapter onwards we'll talk about the mortals; the heroes. After the age of the gods it was the heroes who captured the hearts of men. The gods of Greek mythology were strong and powerful but they also had dubious characters. Zeus for example was always running after one or the other woman. The heroes on the other hand were mortals with outstanding character and sometimes with strength equal to gods. They were sent out on dangerous quests or to solve problems between gods. They could go where the gods couldn't. They started an age when the Greeks began believing that men could be as great as gods.

Chapter 4

The Twelve Labors of Heracles

The Twelve Labors of Heracles

Heracles, or Hercules in Roman, is probably the most famous of all Greek heroes. He was sired by Zeus through a mortal mother, Alcmene. His heroism was evident even as a baby. The jealous mistress, Hera sent two snakes to kill him while Heracles was still a baby. Baby Heracles was found prattling happily with a strangled snake in each hand. As a toddler he was continuously the target of Hera's wrath.

Athena brought baby Heracles to Hera under the pretext that he was an abandoned child. Out of pity, Hera nursed him unaware of his real identity. Heracles suckled so hard on Hera's breasts that it caused her pain. She pushed him away and the sprayed milk formed the Milky Way. He grew up to be the strongest man in the world.

Along with great strength he also had great intellect and when he couldn't do something using his might, he used his brain instead. This is evident from the time when he tricked Atlas into taking back the sky from him. But sometimes his pride and self confidence blinded him. He once threatened to shoot the sun because the temperature was too high. He was also turned mad by Hera several times. That coupled with his quick-fire emotions got him into more trouble than he ever bargained for.

Entering manhood, Heracles had already proved beyond doubt that he was an expert marksman and an accomplished warrior. He considered himself to be as strong as the gods and didn't fear even the gods. After all, it was the gods who needed his help to defeat the Giants. When he was eighteen he killed the Thespian lion all by himself and from then on wore its skin as a cape. He also carried a club and a powerful bow and arrow.

He got married to King Creon's daughter, Megara. In a fit of wrath induced by Hera, he killed his own children. To atone for his sin he was asked to serve King Eurystheus for ten years, performing any task that the king might give him, one for each year. Later the king tricked him into performing two more tasks. These came known as the twelve labors of Heracles.

Eurystheus had become king in place of Heracles due to a cunning plot hatched by Hera when Heracles was not even born. Hera made Zeus promise that the next member of the Perseus family would become the high king. This position was entitled to be Heracles'. Hera sought the help of Ilithiya and slowed down the birth of Heracles and his twin brother. Meanwhile, she made sure that Eurystheus, also a member of the Perseus family was born prematurely. Heracles wouldn't have been born at all if Alcmene's servant hadn't tricked Ilithiya into believing that Alcmene had already given birth.

When Heracles came to Eurystheus to atone for killing his wife and children, Hera made Eurystheus give him impossible tasks hoping that he would be killed in trying to complete them but Heracles managed to complete all 12 labors.

The Twelve Labors

The first labor was to kill the Nemean Lion. This task was supposed to be impossible because the great lion was immune to all weapons known to man. Heracles killed the lion by choking it with his bare hands. He then carried the dead body into Mycenae on his shoulders.

The second labor was to kill Hydra, the creature with 9 heads. The problem was that when one of the heads of Hydra was chopped off, two grew in its place. Heracles was helped in this task by Iolaus who gave him the burning brand he used to sear the neck of the monster to prevent new heads from growing.

The third labor was to capture alive the stag of Artemis which had golden horns. Since this task was not to kill but to capture alive, it took Heracles a long time but he finally managed to capture the beast after a year.

The fourth labor was to capture the Erymanthian Boar. The giant boar lived on Mount Erymanthus. Heracles chased it till it was exhausted and then captured it by driving it into deep snow.

By this time Hera and Eurystheus were getting hopeless and so gave him a truly impossible task. Heracles' fifth labor was to clean the stables of Augeas in one day. The Augean stables were huge and had thousands of cattle and hadn't been cleaned for years. This task didn't require strength but just time and they gave him so less time that he was sure to fail. But Heracles once again used his strength and diverted the flow of two rivers into the stables which caused a flood and cleaned the stables in no time at all.

The sixth labor was to kill the Stymphalian Birds. These were man eating birds that had bronze beaks and metal wings that they could shoot at humans. The problem was that they lived in a marsh and Heracles couldn't reach their nesting site because the marshy ground couldn't hold his weight. Athena helped him by giving him a rattle that was made by Hephaestus. He used the rattle to scare the birds and as they flew out of the marsh he killed them with his arrows that he had dipped in the poisonous blood of Hydra.

The seventh labor was to bring the Cretan Bull that Poseidon had given to Minos. Heracles was able to master the bull and brought him to Eurystheus in a boat.

The eighth labor was to steal the mares of King Diomedes of Thrace. Instead of stealing the mares, Heracles killed Diomedes and then drove the mares to Eurystheus without any opposition.

The ninth labor was to bring back the girdle of the queen of the Amazons, Hippolyta. At first Hippolyta was kind to Heracles and told him that he could have her girdle but Hera interfered and the rest of the Amazon women thought that Heracles was going to kidnap their queen. They attacked him and he fought all of them and killed Hippolyta, thinking that she had ordered the attack. He was able to fight the rest and get away with the girdle.

The tenth labor was to steal the cattle of Geryon. Geryon was a monster living on Erythia and had three bodies attached to a pair of legs. Heracles crossed the Libyan desert to reach the island of Erythia and that's when he was so enraged at the heat that he threatened to shoot an arrow at the sun. Helios was so impressed by his courage that he lent him his chariot on which he rode to the island. On the island first he killed the two headed watch dog of Geryon, Orthrus. Then he killed the monster with his arrows that were dipped in the blood of the Hydra.

The tenth labor was yet not complete because he had to bring the cattle back to Eurystheus and on his way he had more adventures. Hera sent a gadfly to bite the cattle and scatter them and Heracles had to search for them for a long time to gather them all. Then Hera sent a flood and raised the level of a river so that the cattle could not cross. Heracles piled stones in the river till the river bed reached high enough for the cattle to cross. Finally he managed to bring the cattle to Eurystheus who promptly sacrificed the cattle to Hera to appease her.

The eleventh labor was to retrieve the golden apples that grew in the gardens of Hera. They were tended by the Hesperides. Heracles didn't know where the gardens were but he knew that the Hesperides were the daughters of Atlas. So he went to Atlas and asked him to get the apples for him. Atlas was holding the sky on his shoulders and couldn't move to Heracles offered to hold it for him while he was gone. Atlas saw this as an opportunity to be relieved of his punishment and agreed.

Whoever took the burden of carrying the sky on his own volition would have to hold it forever unless someone else offered to take over. Atlas returned with the apples but did not take back the sky. He offered to take the apples to Eurystheus himself. At this point Heracles could not use his might as all of his strength was being used to hold up the sky so he had to rely completely on his own wits. He told Atlas that he agreed with his plan but he just wanted to put his cloak on his shoulder as a pad so that he could carry the burden more easily. Atlas was fooled by this demand and took back the sky for a moment to let Heracles adjust his cloak but instead Atlas took the apples and ran off with them.

The twelfth and last labor required Heracles to go down into the netherworld and retrieve Cerberus, the three headed dog of Hades. This was supposed to be an impossible task as well but Heracles managed to complete it. He went down and even freed Theseus from the chair of forgetfulness. Hades agreed to let him take his dog on the condition that he didn't use any of his weapons to subdue the dog. Heracles managed to tame the monstrous dog using just his hands and his cloak as a shield. He carried the dog up to earth and to Eurystheus. Eurystheus did not want anything to do with the dangerous dog and asked Heracles to return it to Hades. And with this last task, Heracles managed to repent for his sins.

More Adventures

Hercules continued to have adventure after adventure through out his life. He defeated Antaeus, a giant who gained his strength from the earth, in a wrestling match. Antaeus rose up stronger every time Heracles threw him on the ground so he raised the giant into the air, away from the earth and then choked him. He was also part of the crew of Argo, also known as the Argonauts, although he soon abandoned them and didn't participate in the rest of the adventures of the Argonauts.

He also fought the river god Achelous to win the hand of Deianira. He sacked Troy with a few of his friends. He freed Prometheus from his chains in the Caucasus after killing the eagle which tormented Prometheus. He even wrestled Thanatos, the god of death, to bring back his friend's dead wife.

Death

How his death came about is also an interesting story. After winning the hand of his wife Deianira, he was taking her home when they reached a deep river. She couldn't cross it but a centaur named Nessus offered to carry her across on his back. While Heracles was still in the river, the centaur jumped across to the other side and tried to run off with his wife. Heracles shot him with the arrow dipped in hydra's blood and he died. But before dying, he took revenge by giving his now poisoned blood to Deianira and telling her that if she ever needed to cast a love spell on Heracles she should use his blood.

A little while later, Heracles captured a kingdom and sent home some slaves including the princess Iole. Deianira felt insecure by her beauty and decided to use the love charm on Heracles. She sent him a robe on which she sprayed the centaur's blood. As soon as Heracles wore the robe, the hydra's poison started acting on him. But instead of killing him instantly like it did to other mortals, it only caused him a lot of pain but didn't kill him.

In the end Heracles built a funeral pyre for himself, to escape from the unbearable pain. While his mortal body burned, the immortal part rose to the sky to live with the gods. Heracles was the first hero with a mortal parent to be made a god after his death.

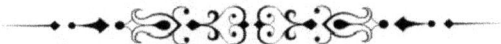

Chapter 5

Achilles and the Trojan War

Achilles and the Trojan War

Achilles was the greatest warrior of Greek mythology. He was the son of King Peleus of the Myrmidons and Thetis, the leader of the 50 Nereids. Both Zeus and Poseidon desired the beautiful sea goddess but were warned by the Titan Prometheus that any male child born to her would become greater than his father. As such, both the brothers ceased their pursuit of her and convinced Peleus to marry her instead.

When Achilles was born, Thetis wanted to gift him with immortality. She took him to the Underworld and holding him by the ankle, dipped him in the waters of the River Styx. However, she was not aware that his only mortal spot on his entire body was the one ankle she had held when she submerged him in the river.

Another version tells that in order to make Achilles immortal, she smothered his body with ambrosia and then placed him on top of a fire to burn away the mortal parts of his body. As she was doing this, however, Peleus interrupted her and enraged, she left them both, with the process unfinished.

The epic poem, *Iliad,* written by Homer sometime in the 8th century BCE, tells us most of what we know about Achilles as one of the central Greek characters that journeyed to Troy to bring back Helen to her husband, King Menelaus.

Prophesies

Achilles' story starts with a few prophesies. The first prophecy of course was the one which brought about his birth; that he would be greater than his father. This led to Zeus and Poseidon backing down and Peleus, who was a hero himself, becoming his father.

When he was born it was prophesized that Achilles would either live a long and healthy life but that it will be boring and devoid of any glory, or that he would have a lot of adventures and die young but receive the glory of being the greatest warrior ever. His mother Thetis wanted him to have a long life even if it wasn't glorious.

The problem was that a third prophecy told Menelaus and Agamemnon that they would never win the Trojan War without the help of Achilles. Thetis didn't want him to go to war as he was still a 15 year old teenager. She hid him in Skyros at the court of king Lycomedes disguised as a girl along with the other daughters of the king. It was Odysseus who went there disguised as a merchant with a lot of jewelry and ornaments. He also had a shield and spear in his wares. All the other girls were busy with the trinkets but one girl gravitated towards the weapons and that's how he found Achilles.

The Trojan War

The beginning of the Trojan War also has an interesting story. Zeus was told that just like he had overthrown his father Cronus, and his father had overthrown his grandfather Uranus, he too would be overthrown by his own son. He was worried because he had so many sons, many of whom were great heroes. He was also worried about the population growth of the humans and so he planned a scheme to start the Trojan War.

He invited all the gods to the wedding of Peleus and Thetis, the parents of Achilles. All except Eris, the goddess of discord, were welcome. Hermes was ordered to stop Eris from entering the banquet because she might cause discord at the wedding. Offended by this, Eris threw a golden apple from outside the door of the hall with the inscription "to the fairest" written on it.

Hera, Athena and Aphrodite all claimed the apple as they believed that they were the fairest. They asked Zeus to decide but he refused to get involved. No god was willing to resolve the issue as they were afraid that no matter who they picked, the other two would get mad. Zeus sent the three goddesses to Paris.

Paris too was unable to decide at first and said that all three were equally fair. The goddesses decided to bribe Paris. Hera promised him great political power, Athena promised him wisdom and great skill in battle and Aphrodite promised him the hand of most beautiful woman on earth, Helen of Sparta. Paris thus decided that Aphrodite was the fairest of all.

When Paris went to Sparta, Aphrodite made Helen fall in love with him and he absconded with her back to Troy. Menelaus decided to take revenge and asked his brother Agamemnon to help him. He also called all the heroes of the Greek world to help him. They all had sworn to protect the marriage of Helen and Menelaus and had to fulfill their oaths. This laid the foundation of the Trojan War.

The Trojan War was the greatest battle in Greek mythology. It lasted for more than 10 years. Many great heroes fought and were killed during the war. Many of them suffered harsh consequences after the war because of offending one or the other gods. Even the gods were divided between the Trojans and the Achaeans.

Achilles in the Trojan War

When the Trojan War began, Achilles was given the command of fifty ships, each containing 50 men. He engaged the services of five commanders-in-chief - Menesthius, Eudorus, Peisander, Phoenix and Alcimedon. After they set sail for Troy, they accidently landed in Mysia where King Telephus ruled. A fight broke out with Achilles wounding Telephus, but the injury wouldn't heal so Telephus consulted an oracle. He was told that only the person who caused the wound would be able to heal it. Telephus went to Achilles and was healed in exchange for directions to Troy.

After reaching Troy, Achilles led many victories over the allies of Troy. The Achaeans were not able to breach the Trojan wall and so they raided the nearby cities and islands that supported Troy and Achilles led these battles gloriously.

The *Iliad* begins the narrative of the Trojan War when King Agamemnon attained a woman named Chryseis and made her his slave. Her father was a priest of the god Apollo and pleaded with him to aid his cause. Upon hearing this, Apollo sent a plague to curse the Greeks. Calchas knew that Apollo was mad about the priest's daughter but he was afraid of telling this to Agamemnon. Achilles promised to protect him and so Calchas informed Agamemnon about Apollo's wrath and how to appease him he had to let go of Chryseis.

Reluctantly, Agamemnon agreed to give up Chryseis but only on the condition that Achilles hand his woman Briseis over to him. Achilles had captured Briseis but had fallen in love with her and was outraged at the lack of respect and withdrew from the battle. He visited with his mother, Thetis, and convinced her to ask Zeus to aid the Trojans so that Agamemnon could realize that he couldn't defeat the Trojans without Achilles.

After this, the Trojans were able to push the Greeks back to the shore. Agamemnon was pressurized by his other commanders to give up Briseis and make peace with Achilles. In the end he did that and also gave more gifts to Achilles, but he stayed firm on not helping them anymore.

Patroclus, the beloved friend of Achilles, donned his armor without him knowing and commanded the Myrmidons in a battle against the Trojans. He fought well and was able to push them back and regain the shore. However, he was slain by Hector, one of King Priam's sons. Hector took Achilles' armor with him and left Patroclus' body there. Achilles was enraged at Patroculus' death. He decided to rejoin the Greeks on the battlefield and kill Hector. Thetis asked Zeus to build new armor for Achilles. Zeus had it made by Hephaestus and this one included the famous shield and spear of Achilles.

He rejoined battle and drove the Trojans back inside their walls and then demanded that Hector fight him in one on one combat. Some sources say that Hector did not want to fight him and Achilles chased him around the Trojan wall three times. Athena then dupes Hector by coming to him in the form of his brother, Deiphobus, and persuading him that he must fight Achilles. Hector fought Achilles and was killed by him. Subsequently, Achilles tied Hector's body to his chariot and dragged it throughout the funeral games held for his friend, Patroclus.

The *Iliad* doesn't recount how Achilles dies. But from other sources we know that Hector prophesized Achilles' death with his last breath. It was Hector's brother, Paris, who shot at the Greek hero, and the poisoned arrow managed to land in

Achilles' only mortal spot – his heel. Other accounts state that Apollo guided the arrow towards Achilles' heel. His body was cremated and his ashes were merged with the ashes of Patroclus.

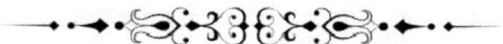

Chapter 6

Atalanta: The Female Hero

Atalanta: The Female Hero

There are two characters from ancient Greek mythology bearing the name of Atalanta; to a number of writers they are both the same person, although others distinguish between them. The general legends tell of the differences between the Arcadian Atalanta and the Boeotian Atalanta.

In the Arcadian version, Atalanta was the daughter of King Iasus (or Iasion) and Clymene. However, when he learnt that his child was female and not the son he had wished for, Iasus abandoned her on the Parthenian Hill (the Virgin Hill), near a cave entrance. She was rescued by a she-bear that raised her in the forest. The bear made her strong and tough and when she was a little older, a group of hunters found her and raised her as their own. They taught her how to hunt and soon she became the better than all of them.

Legends tell that she wore the emblem of Artemis and decided to remain a virgin. She had no interest in men or marriage. Once when two centaurs, tried to capture and rape her, she killed them swiftly with her arrows.

Calydonian Boar Hunt

Next she participated in the Calydonian Boar Hunt. The boar was sent as a punishment by Artemis on King Oineus, who forgot to honour her during a ritual sacrifice. It was a giant beast that no one could catch or kill. It destroyed fields and houses and killed many men and women. It wreaked havoc and so the hunt was declared to kill the boar. All the greatest hunters and heroes gathered to participate in it. So it was natural that Atalanta would also show up there. But her presence wasn't appreciated by the other hunters who felt it beneath them to participate in a hunt with a woman.

Meleager, the son of King Oineus, fell in love with her at first sight and convinced the rest of the heroes and hunters to let her participate. It turned out that she was a better hunter than all of them and was the first one to draw blood from the boar. Meleager than finished the boar with his spear. But he believed that the honour of the hunt should go to Atalanta as she was the one to land the first blow on the boar.

He presented her with the head of the boar but this displeased his uncles who felt that the head should remain with Meleager and the family as a symbol of their great victory. The disagreement got so big that Meleager killed his own uncles.

Now what you need to know is that when Meleager was born, the fates appeared and told a prophecy. They said that they had given him as much life as the time it would take for all the wood burning in the hearth to turn into ash. Hearing this, his mother secretly took out a piece of wood from the hearth and hid it. Since the wood never burned out completely, Meleager stayed alive. But after hearing that his son had killed her brothers over some huntress, she got enraged and threw the piece of wood in the fire. As the wood turned to ashes, Meleager ran out of life and his dream of marrying Atalanta could never come true.

The Footrace

After the boar hunt, she participated in more adventures. She defeated Peleus in a wrestling match at the funeral games for Pelias. One myth tells that she was able to call forth a spring from the rocks near the Cyphanta ruins by hitting it with her spear. She is also said to have participated in the adventures of the Argonauts as the only female on the ship. But other versions say that she was persuaded by Jason to not join his crew as the presence of a female on the ship with so many men would lead to discord between them.

Eventually, King Iasus acknowledged her as his daughter and wanted her to marry. She agreed but only on the condition that every suitor had to compete with her in a footrace. If he could beat her then she would marry him but if he couldn't, then she would kill him. She set this challenge as she was the fastest runner in the human world and because the oracle at Delphi had warned her not to marry. Many men tried to defeat her but she was too fast for all of them and they ended up losing their lives.

Finally Meilanion accepted the challenge. Knowing that he couldn't win against her in a straight footrace, he prayed to the goddess Aphrodite and asked for her help. She presented him with three golden apples that were irresistibly beautiful. When the race began, Atalanta took over him at once as he had expected but he rolled a golden apple in front of her and she bent down to pick it up. This gave him a chance to catch up. Then he threw the second apple a little to the side and when she bent down to pick it up, he gained a lead but she soon caught up to him. He threw the third apple further to the side in the grass along the race track. She left the track to pick up the apple and thus Meilanion won the race and won her hand.

But after winning her hand in marriage, he forgot to thank Aphrodite for her help and she got offended. So she turned them both into lions. This was a curse because the Greeks believed that lions did not mate with other lions but only with leopards. Another version says that when they kissed in the sacred grove of Zeus, he got offended and transformed them into lions.

Some accounts claim Atalanta was the mother of Parthenopaeus by the god of war, Ares, whilst other sources state Meilanion was the father.

In the Boeotian version, there are some similarities and a few discrepancies. Here, she is named the daughter of Schoenus and was the wife of Hippomenes. The footrace was transferred to Onchestus and when he won the race the same way Meilanion did, the two were married in a temple of Cybele. When they kissed, they were instantly transformed into lions and the goddess tied them to her chariot.

In both versions, the reason for their transformation was due to the challenger's neglect to thank Aphrodite for her help in securing Atalanta's hand.

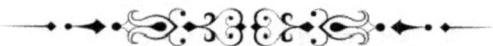

Chapter 7

Bellerophon and Pegasus

Bellerophon and Pegasus

Bellerophon was one of the great Greek heroes but, like many other heroes of his age, fell from grace. He was the son of Poseidon and Eurynome, the wife of Glaucus (other versions state King Glaucus and Eurynome, and the grandson of Sisyphus). His original name was Hipponous but was given the name Bellerophon or Bellerophontes from having killed the aristocratic Corinthian, Bellerus. It is also said that when Perseus beheaded Medusa, from her neck were born two beings. One was the winged horse Pegasus and the other was Chrysaor, which seems to be another name for Bellerophon. This makes him and Pegasus, brothers.

The myth of Bellerophon tells about his killing of Chimera with the help of Pegasus. As a son of Poseidon, Bellerophon was interested in horses and capturing Pegasus was a challenge he eagerly took on. He tried to capture the creature but failed every time. He went and asked for advice from the sage, Polyeidus. The wise sage told him to spend the night in the temple of Athena which he did. During the night, he dreamt about the goddess who presented him with a beautiful golden magical bridle. With this he was able to capture Pegasus. Victorious, he went and asked King Pittheus for his daughter's hand in marriage. However, before he could marry Aethra, Bellerophon killed someone – possibly one of his siblings – and was exiled for his crime.

Bellerophon journeyed to the kingdom of King Proteus to repent for his crime. The king cleansed him of his crime. His wife, Queen Stheneboea, fell in love with Bellerophon and tried to seduce him but he refused her. Angered about his dismissal, Stheneboea lied to her husband, telling him that Bellerophon had tried to make advances on her.

Harming a guest was considered an insult against the gods and so King Proteus looked for ways to get rid of Bellerophon without having to accuse him openly. Instead, he gave him a sealed letter to give to his father-in-law, King Iobates and sent him to his father-in-law.

Bellerophon travelled to Iobates' kingdom on the back of Pegasus and was welcomed with open arms. The king dined with Bellerophon for 9 days before reading the letter. When Iobates read the letter and discovered his daughter's accusations against the young Bellerophon, it put Iobates in a tricky situation as with Proteus in regards to harming a guest.

Killing Chimera

Iobates came up with a solution. Instead of harming Bellerophon outright, he would send him out on a series of heroic quests. The first task given to him was to kill the dreaded monster, Chimera. Chimera was a monster that had the head of a lion, a body of a goat and a snake for a tail. It breathed fire and no one could even approach the monster because of the intense heat of the fire.

Using Pegasus and his bow and arrows, he tried to kill Chimera from the air but failed because the beast's breath was so hot that he couldn't get close enough, even from the air. So Bellerophon came up with an idea. He stuck a block of lead to his spear and flew above Chimera. When the monster breathed fire at him, Bellerophon dropped the lead into the monster's mouth. The heat of the fire melted the lead and it got lodged in the monster's throat, choking it to death.

Next, he was sent to the land of the Solymi, the neighbors and enemies of Iobates. Again, he was able to defeat them and upon his return, was sent off to fight the Amazons. Bellerophon made sacrifices and offerings to the gods, ensuring the gods' favor. He won against the Amazons and upon the knowledge of his victory Iobates arranged his warriors to ambush him. Bellerophon killed every last soldier.

It was at this point that King Iobates realized his mistake – Bellerophon was favored by the gods and harming the young hero would mean risking their wrath. To make amends, Iobates gave Bellerophon half his kingdom and his daughter Philonoe in marriage.

Again, the accounts differ as to what happens to Stheneboea. One version tells that Bellerophon sought revenge on his wife's sister by taking her on a ride on Pegasus and when they were high enough, pushed her off and let her fall. Another version says that upon hearing Bellerophon had married her sister, she realized that her deception would be uncovered and so she killed herself to avoid the shame.

Flying to Olympus

Bellerophon enjoyed a wonderful, happy life with his wife who bore him two sons, Isander and Hippolochus, and two daughters, Laodameia and Deidameia. He performed great heroic deeds and the people adored him as their king.

However, Bellerophon became arrogant and conceited. The love and adoration of his family and people wasn't enough. He decided that he would fly up to the heavens on Pegasus and see the gods. The gods were not impressed and Zeus sent a gadfly to intercept him. The gadfly stung Pegasus and Bellerophon fell but did not die. Instead, he became a cripple and for the rest of his life, he wandered around the world. Pegasus however reached Mount Olympus and Zeus kept him as a bearer of his thunderbolts. Because Bellerophon had offended the gods, no one came to his aid. He eventually died alone.

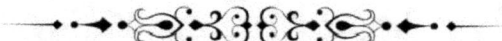

Chapter 8

The Dioscuri

The Dioscuri

The twin brothers, Castor and Pollux (also known as Polydeuces) were called the Dioscuri. They were the sons of Leda but it is generally accepted that they had different fathers. King Tyndareus of Sparta was the father of Castor, the mortal son, and Pollux was the son of Zeus (hence a demi-god), who had seduced the beautiful queen by taking the form of a swan. Accounts vary, with the Dioscuri being born from an egg, together with their twin sisters Helen and Clytemnestra.

There are a few versions that vary as to whom was the son of whom. Homer states that Zeus visited her in the form of a swan and loved her before her husband embraced her – from these unions, Castor and Pollux were sons of Tyndareus whereas only Helen was the child of Zeus; other versions state the twin boys were both the sons of Zeus, the daughters were that of her husband; and another claim Pollux and Helen were the children of Zeus. The most popular version states that Castor was born mortal whereas Pollux was a demi-god, enjoying immortality.

Growing up, the Dioscuri engaged in many feats and expeditions, even taking part in Jason's quest for the Golden Fleece as two of the Argonauts. When they arrived back in Iolcus, they helped Jason take revenge on King Pelias, Jason's uncle, for the murder of his parents and stealing the throne. They also participated in the Calydonian boar hunt, and when their sister, Helen, was kidnapped by King Theseus of Attica, they attacked his kingdom. In return, they kidnapped Aethra, Theseus' mother, and brought her back to Sparta where she was made Helen's slave.

The Fight with Lynceus and Idas
Another popular legend involving the Dioscuri was in relation to the Leucippides. They were the nieces of Leucippus, named Phoebe and Hilaeira, and were the consorts of Lynceus and Idas, who were the cousin brothers of Castor and Pollux. The Dioscuri fell in love with them and kidnapped the two sisters, bringing them back to Sparta and beginning a family dispute.

In retaliation, the cousins attacked a region of Arcadia and stole some cattle from the twins. When the cousins visited their uncle's palace, the Dioscuri, Helen and Paris were there. Knowing the cousins were too busy, the twins decided that this would be the ideal time to take back their cattle and left the palace. This left Helen and Paris alone, ultimately bringing about the start of the Trojan War.

The twin brothers reached the place where their cousins had hidden the cattle. Castor climbed a tree to keep watch while Pollux released the cattle. Lynceus and Idas were on their way back and Lynceus had the ability to see in the dark. He was able to see Castor hiding in the tree before Castor could see them in the dark. The cousins understood what was going on and ambushed Castor. Idas mortally wounded Castor but before that Castor was able to call out to Pollux. A battle ensued and Pollux killed Lynceus. Idas was about to kill Pollux but Zeus was watching everything and struck Idas with his lightning bolt to save his son. Idas was killed instantly.

Pollux asked Zeus to gift Castor with immortality. Zeus gave Pollux the option of sharing his immortality with his brother which he agreed to. From then on, the pair became both immortal and dead. They alternated between Olympus and Hades and represented immortality and death.

They are considered to be patrons of travellers and sailors. The two brightest stars in the constellation of Gemini are said to be the Dioscuri. They are often represented with horses and skull caps which are said to be the eggshells out of which they were born. They are also patrons of athletes and boxers.

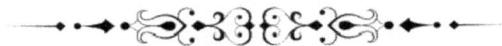

Chapter 9

Jason and the Golden Fleece

Jason and the Golden Fleece

The ancient legend of Jason and the Golden Fleece has been retold for more than 3000 years and is one of the most popular classical myths. The quest for the Golden Fleece is a tale of hardship, challenges, a sea voyage into lands unknown to acquire a magical item in order to take back his throne in Iolcus from his uncle, King Pelias.

The myth is placed around 1300 BCE, a generation before the Trojan War starts, but it makes its first appearance in the 8th/9th centuries, around the time of Homer. It originated in Thessaly and has been retold several times by various ancient writers, including Apollodorus of Rhodes, Hyginus and Ovid. Apollodorus' version is the one retold the most and a copy was held in the Library of Alexander in Egypt. It changed for various reasons, from turbulent political issues in the 5th century BCE, to artistic and scientific reasons.

The Background of the Golden Fleece

A long time before the time of Jason, there was a king named Athamas. He had a wife called Nephele and two children; Prince Phrixus and Princess Helle. He got married to another woman called Princess Ino. Nephele rightfully felt that Ino would try to kill her son so that her own son would grow up to become king. Nephele was right because Ino made a plan for killing Phrixus.

Somehow Ino got hold of all the seed corn and parched it so that when it was sowed, nothing grew out of it. The entire crop failed and the kingdom faced a drought. The king sent a messenger to the oracle to find out what had happened and how to remedy it. But the young queen bribed the messenger so that when he returned he told the king that the oracle had told him that the corn would not grow ever again, unless the king sacrificed the young prince.

The people of the kingdom pressurised him and he felt like he had no choice. Nephele prayed to the gods to save her son. In answer, Hermes sent a ram with a shinning golden fleece that rescued the young prince as well as his sister from the sacrificial alter. For some reason the sister was also being sacrificed but the ram saved them both. The golden ram (also known as Chrysomallus) flew over the seas with the two children on the back but somehow Helle fell into the water in the narrow strait that divided Europe and Asia. Since then that strait is known as Hellespont or the strait of Helle.

The ram took Phrixus to Colchis, a country beyond the unfriendly sea (the black sea) where king Aeetes raised him like his own and even let him marry his own daughter. Phrixus sacrificed the golden ram to thank Zeus and the other gods. The Golden Fleece was given as a gift to Aeetes who kept it in a sacred grove guarded by a serpent also known as the Colchan Dragon. An oracle foretold that should the Golden Fleece ever be taken, Aeetes would lose his crown.

The Beginning of Jason's Quest

The legend begins at the kingdom of Iolcus (near modern day Volos in Greece) when Pelias, Jason's uncle, took his brother's throne by force and exiled the young boy and his parents. Jason was sent to Mount Pelion in Thessaly, where he was raised by the wise and gentle centaur, Chiron, who raised many Greek heroes. During this time, an oracle told King Pelias that if he ever met a man wearing a single sandal, he would lose his throne.

When Jason was 20 years old, he made his way to his uncle's kingdom. On the way he saw an old woman and helped her, losing a sandal in the process of crossing the river. The old woman turned out to be the goddess Hera. Jason made his way to Iolcus and announced who he was to Pelias, making his case regarding taking back the throne for himself. Pelias deliberated and then told Jason that if he wanted to take the throne, first he had to acquire the Golden Fleece and bring it back to him. Only then would he give the throne to Jason. The young hero was excited by the prospect of adventure so he agreed and began to prepare for his quest.

Jason began preparations for the journey, first by creating a mighty ship which was known as the Argo. He called all the noble and heroic young men from all over Greece. Hera helped him by stirring the hearts of the heroes to join his quest. At first, 50 heroes began on the voyage and later this number increased to 100 and included many Greek heroes including Heracles, the Dioscuri, Meleager, Peleus, Telamon, Orpheus and the only female hero, Atalanta. They were called the Argonauts. Historically, Jason's journey was considered to be the first major long-distant sea voyage undertaken in the ancient Greek world.

Lemnos

Jason and the Argonauts first landed on the island of Lemnos, located in the northeast of the Aegean Sea. When they arrived they noticed that there were only women on the island. These women had been cursed by Aphrodite because they forgot to worship her. The curse made them stink really badly which made their husbands seek other women and abandon them. The women then killed their husbands in revenge.

The king, Thoas, was saved by his daughter, Hypsipyle. She set him off the island in a hollow chest and he made it to a safer shore. Since then the women lived alone on the island till the Argonauts arrived. The women mated with the heroes and created the race called Minyae. Jason had twins with Hypsipyle. Later it was Heracles who persuaded the Argonauts to move on with their quest.

Historically Lemnos was famous in the ancient world for producing purple cloth by using certain species of shellfish. The process was incredibly smelly and is probably a way of explaining why no one apart from the dye makers stayed on the island.

Cyzius

After Lemnos, the Argonauts landed in the land of the Doliones. Their king, Cyzius, welcomed the heroes. He told them about the Bear Mountain where the crew went to search for supplies. The king didn't tell them about the Gegeines who lived in the forests beyond the Bear Mountain. These were a fierce race of giants with six hands and leather loincloths.

The Gegeines watched most of the crew enter the forest and then attacked the ship. Heracles was guarding the ship and managed to kill most of the giants before Jason and the crew returned. They killed the rest of the giants and then set sail.

A little further on, they stopped again and sent more men into the forest to get fresh water and other supplies. One of these was Hylas, the companion of Heracles. Hylas was very good looking and while he was gathering fresh water from a stream, a water nymph was attracted to him. The nymph took hold of him and dragged him deep into the water.

When Hylas didn't return, Heracles went out in search of him. He was so saddened at the loss of the boy that he forgot all about the Argonauts and continued to search for the boy for a long time. From there the Argonauts went ahead without Heracles.

The Argonauts set sail again but lost their bearings and returned to the land of the Doliones at night. In the darkness, the Doliones thought that they were some enemies who had attacked their land. They weren't expecting the heroes to return. A fight broke out and the heroes killed many men, including King Cyzius. In the morning they realized their mistake and held a funeral for the good king.

Phineas and the Harpies

Next they came upon a land where an old prophet called Phineas lived. Apollo had given him the gift of prophecy and he foretold the things that Zeus was going to do. This displeased Zeus and he set the Harpies on him. The Harpies were vicious creatures with wings, hooked beaks and sharp claws. They also left a strong stench when they left a place.

Whenever the old man sat down to eat, the Harpies would descend on him and snatch his food. Whatever food was left behind would stink so badly that no man could eat it. This led to the old man becoming extremely weak and thin. Jason took pity on Phineas and decided to help him.

They sat down to eat together and when the Harpies descended, the Argonauts fought with them. The Harpies couldn't handle so many great heroes and tried to escape. But among the Argonauts were the sons of Boreas, the god of the North Wind. They could fly and they chased the Harpies into the sky. Before they could kill the Harpies, Iris, the goddess of the rainbow and the messenger of the gods came down and stopped them. She brought the message that Zeus had lifted his curse and the Harpies would never torture the old man again.

The Symplegades

As a thanks Phineas gave them good advice about their future. He told them how to cross the Symplegades or the Clashing Rocks. These were huge rocky cliffs at the mouth of the unforgiving sea. They clashed together whenever anyone tried to sail up the sea, crushing the ship.

Phineas told them to first release a dove and if the dove was able to pass the rocks without being crushed, then they could also do it. But if the dove was crushed then they would also be crushed and their quest was doomed.

Jason released the dove and saw that it was able to pass with only a few of its tail feathers caught between the clashing rocks. So they too moved ahead and the Argo was able to pass the rocks with very slight damage to its stern ornament. Since then, the two rocks joined together and stopped clashing. So Jason made the sea safer for all future sailors.

Historically speaking, this part of the myth is an explanation of how the Greeks were first able to sail upstream through the strong currents of the Bosphorus to enter the Black Sea. The Black Sea was no longer called the hostile sea and from then on it was known as the welcoming sea.

Jason and the Argonauts then set sail and had a few more adventures. They landed in Samothrace where they were initiated into the Kabeiroi. This was a cult dedicated to non-Greek gods, perhaps creator or earth/fertility gods, who could offer great protection to the Argonauts. After Samothrace, they journeyed onto Troy and then arrived at the Sea of Marmara the following morning.

Colchis

The relatively easy part of the voyage was over when they landed in Colchis (modern day Georgia). Upon landing, the heroes all sat together and came up with a plan of action. The decided that they should walk to the city, known at that time as Aia, and just meet with the king and ask for the golden fleece. On the way they noticed dead bodies wrapped in hides and hanging from the trees (a practice which occurred in Georgia all the way through to the 17th century).

Jason arrived at the palace of King Aeetes and asked him to give him the Golden Fleece. As with Pelias, Aeetes deliberated and agreed to Jason's request but only if he completed a series of tasks. Firstly, he had to harness bronze bulls that bellowed fire and then use them to plough a field and plant dragon's teeth. From these teeth emerged fierce earth-born warriors known as the Sparti. They attacked the nearest man and so he would have to defeat all of them as well.

The tasks were impossible to complete on his own and Jason was trying to figure out a way to complete them. At the same time, Aphrodite struck Medea, the daughter of Aeetes and the high priestess of the goddess Hecate, with an arrow to ensure that she fell in love with Jason. Being a priestess of Hecate, Medea was talented in magic and sorcery. She told Jason that she would help him if he took her back to Iolcus and married her. He agreed to this and she gave him an amulet which would protect him from the immense heat of the fire of the bulls. She also told him that if he can't defeat the Sparti, he should throw a rock in their midst.

He took on the bulls wearing the amulet. It protected him from the fire but he still had to use all his strength to subdue them and yoke them to the plough. After he had sown the dragon's teeth and the warriors sprung from the ground, he did as Medea had suggested and threw a rock in their midst. The Sparti fought each other until they all fell. Jason had managed to do the impossible.

Aeetes had a huge banquet prepared after he realised that Jason had completed his seemingly-impossible set of tasks, but secretly told Medea that he planed to murder Jason and the Argonauts rather than giving them the Golden Fleece. Medea went to Jason and told him what her father planed to do and aided him in securing the Golden Fleece. The fleece was guarded by a fierce dragon; accounts vary but the beast was either put in a magical sleep through Medea's magic or was slain by Jason. Another version says that Jason was eaten by the dragon but then made to disgorge him by either Medea or Aphrodite.

Jason stole the Golden Fleece and along with Medea and the rest of the Argonauts, ran back to the Argo and set sail for home. In a later version it is said that the king chased them and Medea killed her younger brother and cut his body into pieces, scattering the pieces. Aeetes stopped to collect his son's body and the Argo escaped.

The Return Journey

Jason and the Argonauts experienced many adventures on their journey back to Iolcus. Zeus sent a storm as punishment for the killing of her own brother by Medea. It blew the ship of course and no one knew how to get back home. The ship, Argo, then spoke and told the Argonauts that they needed to go to the island of Aeaea and meet the nymph Circe. They did this and after purification of Medea, they could move ahead.

When they were crossing the islands of the Sirens, Orpheus, saved their lives with his lyre. The Sirens sang songs that were so mesmerizing that the sailors were drawn to it and they crashed into the rocks. But when Orpheus heard the song of the Sirens, he began playing music on his lyre. It was sweeter and louder than the song of the Sirens and so the Argonauts were not attracted to the Sirens.

One popular myth tells how they came to the island of Crete but found it was guarded by the giant bronze man, Talos, fashioned by the smith-god Hephaestus. They learnt the only way to defeat him was to inflict a wound on his ankle, his only weak spot. Through Medea's magic, Talos caught his ankle on the rocks and the ichor inside him ran out, effectively killing him.

Jason's Betrayal

When Jason arrived back home with Medea, he found that King Pelias had murdered his father, and his mother had died due to grief. Medea exacted revenge by offering to rejuvenate Pelias but killed him instead. Other versions state that Jason's father didn't die but Medea rejuvenated him through her magic. She offered the same deal to Pelias who accepted; his daughters carried out the procedure on him but Medea gave them the wrong herbs and so he died.

Another version says that Medea approached the daughters of King Pelias and showed them the procedure by carrying it out on an old ram. She put the ram to sleep and then cut it into little pieces. Then she boiled the pieces in water along with some herbs and chanted an incantation. Out of the boiling water jumped forth a young lamb. Then she gave the daughters a potion to put the king to sleep. The daughters then cut their own father and put his pieces in boiling water. But when it was time to recite the incantation, Medea ran away, leaving the daughters in agony over what they had just done.

Either way, Jason and Medea were banished and arrived in Corinth. During this time they had two sons together. In Corinth, Jason was offered the hand of the king's daughter in marriage. And he accepted the offer. This was a huge betrayal for Medea who had not only left her country, betrayed her father and killed her own brother but also killed other people for Jason. Betrayed and angry, Medea poisoned Glauce, Jason's new bride. Accounts vary from this point; the earliest account tells that the Corinthian people were enraged at this and stoned Medea's two sons to death whereas the popular Euripides version states that Medea killed her own children.

Heartbroken and despondent, Jason wandered around Greece for many years before arriving back where the Argo had been beached. It was here that the beam of the Argo broke and fell on top of him, killing Jason instantly.

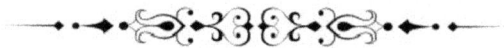

Chapter 10

Odysseus

Odysseus

Odysseus was one of the most popular characters to come out of ancient Greece. He was the central character in Homer's *Odyssey* which was written sometime around the 8th century BCE and was a main character from Homer's first legendary epic poem, *Iliad*. He was the son of Laertes and Anticlea.

Before the Trojan War

Long before the Trojan War began, Odysseus was one of the many suitors who were trying to win Helen in marriage. Helen was the beautiful stepdaughter of King Tyndareus and the daughter of the god Zeus. Although Odysseus was handsome and intelligent, there were far too many suitors for there to be any clear winner. Odysseus went to Tyndareus and told him that he had come up with a fair way of deciding who would marry Helen and he would tell him on the condition that he could marry Penelope, the king's beautiful niece. Tyndareus agreed and Odysseus proposed that they should draw straws to determine who would marry her. But before they did, he made each and every one of the suitors to swear to the gods that they would support the couple throughout their lives no matter what happened to them. This was to ensure that once one of them was chosen, the others could not protest or fight or try to steal Helen. They all agreed and it was Menelaus who pulled out the right straw. Menelaus married Helen and Odysseus married her cousin, Penelope.

Whilst the son of King Priam of Troy, Prince Paris, was in Greece, he and Helen fell in love and he took her to Troy with him. Upon hearing of her abduction, all her previous suitors were brought together and expected to help Menelaus' in the task of bringing her home to Greece. In the meantime, an oracle predicted that should Odysseus join the others then it would be an extremely long time before he would see his family again. In an attempt to get out of the expedition, Odysseus tried to convince the others that he was insane by yoking an ox and a donkey to a plough and sowing the land with salt. Palamedes saw through the deception and placed Odysseus' baby son, Telemachus, in the way of the plough – Odysseus changed route at once and was exposed. Odysseus hated Palamedes from then onwards.

After Odysseus' deception was discovered, the group tried to recruit Achilles. Achilles was the son of the goddess Thetis and she had dressed him up as a young girl in order to stop him from going to war. Two oracles were at play here: an oracle had told the group that they would only win against Troy if Achilles joined them and the second oracle had informed the goddess that her son would either live a long and peaceful existence or else he would die young in a blaze of glory. When they arrived on Scyros, Odysseus attempted to find out which one of the women was Achilles. Odysseus arranged a variety of weapons on a table and only one person was interested in them – Achilles. The battle horn was sounded and Achilles was officially a member of the Greek forces.

During the Trojan War

When the Greeks finally reached Troy and the fight began, Odysseus made himself indispensable as a military strategist and advisor. Right at the beginning, he used his cunning to get things started. An oracle had prophesized that the first Greek to set foot on Trojan soil would be the first one to die so no one was ready to step forward. Odysseus was the first one to jump out of his ship but he had very cleverly thrown his shield down first and he landed on his shield and not on the soil. Protesilaus was the next to jump and the first one to land on Trojan soil. He was the first one to die when he was killed by Hector.

Odysseus kept the Greek's morale high and was able to keep Agamemnon from leaving the war. In addition to this, he was able to calm Achilles down after his beloved friend, Patroclus, was killed by the Trojan prince, Hector.

But Odysseus also had a nasty side. Accounts differ but one version claims that he proved that Palamedes was a traitor to the group and had him stoned to death. In another version, Odysseus convinced him that at the bottom of a well there was a great treasure to be had. Palamedes climbed into the well and when he came to the bottom, Odysseus and Diomedes covered it, burying him alive in the well.

It was the conception and creation of the Trojan Horse which makes Odysseus incredibly famous in the *Iliad*. The Greeks needed a way of breaching the Trojan walls and Odysseus came up with the idea of a giant wooden horse inside which they could hide themselves. They presented it to the Trojans and retreated. The Trojans brought the horse inside the wall and started to celebrate their victory. When night fell and the Trojans were drunk, the Greeks jumped out of the hollow body of the horse and killed the Trojans, effectively winning the war.

But they did not stop there. They ravaged the city, killed everyone and burned the city to the ground. In their hatred, they carried out many atrocities on the Trojans and even disrespected the gods. This resulted in Athena and Poseidon, who supported the Greeks during the war, to get angry. So when the Greeks set sail to get back home, they all faced many dangers and problems and suffered just as they had made the Trojans suffer.

After the Trojan War

From here the story of *Odyssey* begins. Odysseus started to make his way home to Ithaca, a journey which would take him ten years to complete against incredible odds. First, the ship was blown off-course and they landed on the island where the Cyclops lived. Odysseus and his men were caught by the one-eyed giants and taken to

Polyphemus' cave where he intended to eat them. Odysseus was able to trick Polyphemus and blinded him. However, before they escaped, the Cyclops managed to find out his name and told Polyphemus' father, the sea god Poseidon. Because of the injury to his son, Poseidon was determined not to allow Odysseus easy sailing back to Ithaca.

The next stop on Odysseus' journey was reaching the island that belonged to Aeolus, the god of winds. He gave a bag containing all the winds, apart from the west, to Odysseus and the west wind blew them all the way to Ithaca. However, just before they arrived home, one of the crew thought it contained gold or treasure and opened it, allowing the other three winds to escape. The winds carried them all the way back to Aeolus' island but he refused to help them once more, so they parted.

They next arrived at the island of the Laestrygonians. These were a man eating tribe and were able to capture the crews of all the ships, apart from the crew of Odysseus. They departed from the island in haste and arrived on the island of Circe. She was the daughter of the sun god Helios and the sister of King Aeetes and Pasiphae and was an incredibly powerful sorceress. When they arrived, Circe used magical herbs to transform all the crew into pigs but Odysseus was saved by an herb that had been given to him by Hermes. Circe fell madly in love with Odysseus and changed the pigs back into his men. The crew remained on the island for a year (some accounts claim three), with Circe having a son by Odysseus, before they once more departed for Ithaca.

Odysseus and his men reached the edge of the world, journeying into the underworld. The shade (ghost or spirit) of the sage Teiresias advised him what to do and where to go to get back home. Odysseus also met the shade of his mother who advised him that Penelope was being fiercely pursued by suitors. Odysseus left the Underworld and returned back to Circe's island. She gave him invaluable advice on how to avoid the fate bestowed on sailors who pass by the island of the Sirens, as well as avoiding the monsters Scylla and Charybdis.

When they reached the island of Thrinacia, the Greek hero stupidly forgot Circe's advice and seized some cattle which belonged to Helios. Furious, Helios demanded that Zeus punish them otherwise he would make the sun shine deep down in the Underworld. Zeus agreed and caused Odysseus' ship to sink, only permitting the hero to survive. Odysseus washed up on the island of Ogygia where the nymph Calypso lived. She kept him on her island for several years, begetting a son with him, before Hermes convinced her to let him go.

Next Odysseus landed on the island of the Phaeacians (contemporary Corfu) and they aided him in reaching Ithaca. When he arrived in his city it was dark and Athena transformed him into the guise of an old beggar. This way he could understand more about what had transpired since he had been gone. He learned that a lot of suitors had camped up at his home to win Penelope's hand. They had been living off of his estate for many years, eating his food and depleting his stocks. Penelope and her son Telemachus had just managed to restrain the suitors for so long.

But seeing no other option, Penelope had proclaimed she would give herself in marriage to the next man who could string Odysseus' bow and shoot an arrow between 12 axe shafts. The suitors lined up, as did Odysseus in disguise, but none could do it except for this mysterious stranger. When he revealed himself, he was furious at the suitors who had taken advantage of his wife and son. He killed all the suitors, with the help of his son. Despite this, Penelope thought that the man before her could not be Odysseus but a deity in masquerade. In the end, she tested him by requesting that he move their bed into a different room. Odysseus told her that this wasn't possible as one of the legs of the bed was part of a living olive tree.

Later on, the son of Odysseus and Circe, Telegonus, arrived in Ithaca as he wanted to get to know his father. When he arrived he killed some sheep as he was famished. Without realising who each other was, Odysseus and Telegonus fought, with the hero eventually being killed. Telegonus, in recompense, escorted Penelope and Telemachus to his mother. Circe made them both immortal and the two sons of Odysseus married each other's mother.

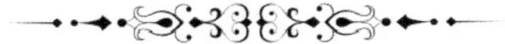

Chapter 11

Peleus

Peleus

Peleus was the son of King Aeacus of Aegina and the nymph Endeis who was either the daughter or granddaughter of the wise centaur, Chiron. He is famous for being the husband of the goddess Thetis and the father of the great Greek hero, Achilles.

There are several myths featuring Peleus. Early in his life, legends say that he killed his half-brother or stepbrother, Phocus; with his brother Telamon whilst they were all hunting (other accounts say that Endeis convinced her sons to kill the boy as she was jealous of him). Peleus and Telamon, wanting to escape punishment, left Aegina and ventured to the land known as Phthia. There he met and fell in love with the daughter of King Eurytion, named Antigone. They had a daughter called Polydora together. When Jason was recruiting for his quest to search for the Golden Fleece, Peleus, Telamon and Eurytion all joined and became part of the Argonauts. When the quest was completed and they returned home, Peleus killed Eurytion whilst out hunting and fled the kingdom.

Next, Peleus came to Iolcus where Astydameia fell head over heels for him. She was the wife of King Acastus but he refused to give into her seductions. In revenge, Astydameia wrote a letter to Antigone saying that Peleus was to marry her daughter. Angered and betrayed, Antigone killed herself. After this, Astydameia went to her husband and informed him that Peleus had tried to rape her. Acastus dragged Peleus to a forest where he was left to be attacked by the fierce centaurs. However, he was rescued by the wise centaur Chiron. Other versions claim the god Hermes helped him. After fleeing from danger, Peleus destroyed the town and murdered both Astydameia and her husband.

Eventually, Peleus came across the beautiful sea goddess Thetis. He tried to win her by capturing her but she was able to transform herself into different shapes and escaped from his clutches. Proetus told Peleus that to win her, he must hold onto Thetis the next time he caught her. When he managed to capture her, she tried to change her shape as usual but he held on no matter how many times she tried to escape. Eventually, she agreed to marry him. At their wedding, the majority of the Olympian gods were welcomed. All except for the goddess of discord, Eris. To seek revenge against the couple for the lack of invitation, she let fall the Apple of Discord amongst the goddesses. It stated "to the fairest". Three of the goddesses – Athena, Aphrodite and Hera – started to bicker about whom it should go to and asked Zeus to pick the right person. Not wanting to argue, he asked Paris, the prince of Troy, to choose instead. Each of the goddesses tried to bribe him but in the end, Paris chose Aphrodite, who promised him the hand of Helen, the most beautiful woman in Greece. Hence, this was the incident which began the Trojan War.

Peleus and Thetis went on to have several sons but the first six died at birth; only Achilles, the seventh child, survived. Peleus sent his son to study under Chiron, the wise Centaur. Peleus was given the immortal horses, Balius and Xanthus, as a marriage present by Zeus. Achilles used these horses and Peleus' spear during his fights.

It is not clear what happened to this hero in the end. Some say that he might have died after his own son, Acastus, exiled him. Another version says that he joined Thetis and was made immortal.

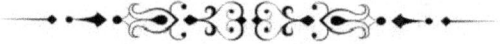

Chapter 12

Perseus and Medusa

Perseus and Medusa

Perseus was one of most beloved Greek heroes in mythology. The legend begins with a king named Acrisius whose daughter, Danae, was incredibly beautiful. Acrisius was informed by the Pythian Oracle that any male child born to Danae would eventually kill him. Trying to avoid this bloody fate, the king locked his daughter up in a bronze tower to ensure that she would never meet a man and have children.

The tower was impregnable for mortal men; it had no doors, just a single small window that Danae could look out of. A shower of gold streamed through the window one evening and made love to her. Danae realized that this was a god but she wasn't certain as to which one it was.

Danae and the god, who happened to be the king of gods, Zeus, begot a male child whom she gave birth to in the tower. When Acrisius discovered that his daughter had given birth, he was furious and ordered the pair of them to be locked in a chest and had it thrown out to sea.

Zeus was angered by the way his lover and child were being treated and had his brother, Poseidon, guide the chest safely to shore. They landed on the island of Seriphos which was ruled by King Polydectes (a later Italian version has them wash up on the Italian coast where Danae married King Pilumnus). A fisherman named Dictys and the king's brother, discovered the chest and opened it, freeing the frightened mother and child. Danae was beautiful and the king wanted to marry her but she refused. Polydectes would have forced her to marry him if it wasn't for Perseus, who had by now grown up into a handsome young man, and so hatched a plan to be free of him.

Another account claims that Polydectes made Danae his slave and tried to seduce her but she refused his advances. So that he could have her undivided attention, he sent Perseus off on a quest to bring back the head of the Gorgon Medusa; when he brought it back he would give Hippodameia to Perseus as a wedding gift.

Another version claims that Danae married Polydectes willingly and together they brought Perseus up into manhood. When Acrisius heard about this, he travelled to Seriphos and informed him about the curse that Perseus was to bring about his death. Polydectes interfered on Perseus' behalf and had Perseus agree not to kill his grandfather. Acrisius tried to return home but fierce storms delayed him and during this time, Polydectes died. At the funeral games, Perseus threw a disc but the winds carried it to Acrisius and killed him, thus completing the prophecy. Perseus then travelled to Argos and took possession of the crown.

The more popular version of the myth says that Polydectes decided that he would hold a fake wedding and pretended to marry a beautiful young lady. All the guests were required to bring a present but Perseus, who was extremely poor, couldn't bring a gift. When Polydectes saw this, he pretended to be angry. After an intense argument, Perseus agreed to bring anything Polydectes asked for, to which Polydectes requested the severed head of the Gorgon Medusa.

Killing Medusa

Perseus set off from his island home and journeyed around Greece for days in the attempt to discover where the Gorgons lived. One night, he was suddenly overcome with just how impossible his quest really was – Medusa was a terrifying monster, once a priestess in the service of Athena before she was seduced by Poseidon and the goddess, in revenge, transformed her into a monster. Her hair was changed into snakes and just looking at her face could turn any man into stone. While he was despairing about the situation, a beautiful woman and young man materialized before him. They were Athena and Hermes. They told him that since he was a son of Zeus and their half-brother, they would aid him. Hermes gave him his winged sandals and the sickle Cronus wielded when he castrated his father, Uranus. Athena presented him with her shield so that he could avoid being turned into stone. In addition, they gave him directions on how to find Medusa's hideout.

Perseus' next stop was to visit the lair of the Graeae, the three hags of fate and the daughters of Zeus born old. There was only one eye and one tooth that were shared between the three women. When Perseus arrived, he saw that one of the women was just about to hand the eye to one of her sisters and Perseus snatched it. He told them he would only give it back to them if they helped him in his quest. The Graeaea said that he should make his way to the Nymphs of the North and acquire two items, a magic bag and a cap which would render him invisible.

Another version state that the Graeaea were the guardians of the Gorgons and he threw their one tooth in the lake so they could no longer protect them.

After gaining these items, Perseus made his way to the lair of the Gorgons. There were three Gorgons, two were immortal and posed no threat, it was only Medusa (who was mortal) that was considered dangerous. Perseus discovered that the sisters were sleeping and, using the shield as a mirror, he cut off Medusa's head with a sickle and put it in the bag given to him by the Nymphs. From the severed head, flew out the flying horse, Pegasus. Despite having been cut off, the head was still powerful enough to turn someone to stone. Medusa's sisters awoke and tried to kill Perseus but using the winged sandals Hermes had given him, Perseus was able to escape.

Other Adventures

Perseus had many adventures on the way back to Seriphus including one with the Titan, Atlas. Zeus had punished him by having him carry the heavens on his shoulders for all eternity. Perseus took out the severed head of Medusa and transformed him to stone in order to relieve him of the immense weight.

Perseus' next stop was in the land of Aethipoia when he discovered what he thought was a statue chained to a rock by the shore. When he ventured closer, he discovered that it was, in fact, a beautiful young woman. He asked her why she was there and she told him that her name was Andromeda and her mother, Queen Cassiopeia, had boasted her daughter's beauty was more than that of the Nereids. Poseidon was furious and demanded Andromeda to be sacrificed to a sea monster. At this time, a huge sea monster rose from the waters and tried to devour the beautiful princess. Perseus took Medusa's head from the bag and turned the monster to stone. Perseus freed Andromeda from her chains and escorted her back to her father, King Cepheus, where he asked him if he could marry her. Cepheus agreed and Andromeda and Perseus were married. With her he became the father of Perses, whom he left with the king when he made his way back home to Seriphos.

As Perseus journeyed back to his hometown, he stopped to take part in some games. He participated in the discus games; only when he threw his, it struck an old man. This turned out to be his grandfather, Acrisius, and therefore completed the prophecy.

Upon arriving in Seriphos, Perseus came across Dictys, the fisherman who had rescued Danae and Perseus from their watery fate. He informed them of Polydectes' wedding deception and that since Danae refused to marry him, he had made her his slave. Perseus vowed revenge and asked Dictys to look after Andromeda whilst he went to the palace.

When Perseus arrived at the palace, he announced that everyone who was a friend of his should avert their eyes. He then took out Medusa's head and transformed Polydectes and his court retinue into stone.

Perseus featured in many more myths and was ultimately killed by the god Dionysus. As a reward for his good deeds, both Perseus and Andromeda were transformed into constellations in the sky.

Chapter 13

Theseus

Theseus

Theseus was the son of Poseidon and Aethra, the wife of the King of Athens, Aegeus. He was one of the most important heroes of Greek mythology and the biggest Athenian hero. There are several myths related to Theseus.

King Aegeus married Aethra, daughter of king Pittheus of Troezen, a small city to the southwest of Athens. On their wedding night Aegeus got drunk and fell asleep. Aethra had received instructions from Athena in a dream and so waded to the nearby island of Sphairia. There Poseidon took Aethra and made her pregnant with Theseus. King Aegeus never found out and instead he left his sword and sandals buried underneath a huge stone and told Aethra that when their son is strong enough to lift the stone, send him to Athens with the sword and sandals. In Athens Aegeus made Medea (Jason's consort who had killed her own children and left Corinth) his consort.

Theseus grew up in Troezen to become a brave and strong young man. He removed the stone and retrieved the sandals and sword and was told about his father's wishes. He decided to leave for Athens but did not go by ship, which was the safest route, but instead through the long land route which was full of perils. He did this because he wanted to prove himself as a brave hero.

The Six Labors

On the way to Athens he killed 6 bandits and beasts that tormented travelers. These are also known as the 6 labors of Theseus. In Epidaurus, he killed the bandit Periphetes who beat his opponents into the ground with his staff. In Isthmian there was a robber named Sinis who tied his victims to two pine trees that were bent towards the ground and then he released the pine trees, ripping his victims in half. Theseus killed him using his own method.

At Crommyon he killed an enormous pig called the Crommyonian Sow. In Megara a robber named Sciron forced travelers along a narrow ledge and told them to wash his feet if they wanted to live. When they knelt in front of him he would kick them off the cliff face and into the sea. Theseus threw Sciron from this same cliff.

The king Cercyon of Eleusis challenged people to a wrestling match. If they won, they would become king and if he won, he would kill them. Theseus accepted the challenge and won and then killed Cercyon. The last bandit was Procrustes near Eleusis who asked people to lie on a bed and if they were too big for it, he would cut off their limbs or if they were too short he would stretch them till they fit. The trick was that he had two different sized beds, so no one ever fit. Theseus cut off his feet with his own axe and killed him.

Marathonian Bull

When he reached Athens, he didn't reveal his true identity to Aegeus but Medea, through her magic, found out that he was the king's son and tried to kill him so that her own son would be left as heir. First she had Theseus capture the Marathonian Bull hoping that he'd die in the attempt but Theseus captured the bull and sacrificed it in Athens. Medea then manipulated Aegeus to poison Theseus by throwing a banquet for him. Just as Theseus was about to drink the poisonous wine, Aegeus recognized his sword and sandals and struck the cup from his hands. Medea fled to Asia.

Minotaur

As the son of king Aegeus and the great hero who had slain several bandits and beasts, Theseus was loved in Athens. His next adventure was the killing of the Minotaur. The story goes like this: King Minos of Crete had a son named Androgeus who came to Athens to take part in the Pan-Athenian games but was assassinated by the Pallantides who were the nephews of Aegeus and were jealous of the popularity Androgeus was getting as an athlete. Minos was greatly angered and attacked Athens. He spared the city on the condition that as retribution, every nine years, 7 young boys and 7 young maidens be sent to Crete to be sacrificed to the Minotaur.

Theseus was present when the third batch was to be sent to Crete and he offered to be one of the 7 boys as he wanted to slay the Minotaur and end this custom. He told his father that when he returns he'll remove the black sail of the ship and hoist the white sail so that he could know that his son was still alive.

In Crete, Ariadne, the daughter of Minos fell in love with him on first sight and decided to help him. The Minotaur was held captive inside a great maze. The victims were thrown into the maze and no one could ever come out of it. Eventually they ran into the Minotaur, who was a man with a bull's head, and he killed and ate them. Ariadne went to Daedalus, the architect of the maze, and asked him how one could come out of the maze. On Daedalus' advice she gave Theseus a ball of thread and told him to tie it to the door of the maze and unwind it as he went deeper into the maze. To come back all he had to do was follow the thread. She did this after making him promise that he would take her to Athens and marry her.

Theseus went in with the ball of thread and found the Minotaur, sleeping at the center of the maze. He woke up and the two had a fight in which Theseus defeated and killed the Minotaur. Some accounts say that he strangled him with his bare hands while others say that he had hid a sword in his tunic. He came out along with the other Athenian boys and girls and all of them fled along with Ariadne and her younger sister Phaedra.

On the way back to Athens, they rested on a small island. While everybody slept, Athena woke Theseus and told him that he must leave Ariadne and Phaedra here and rush back to Athens. Theseus did as the goddess asked but he was grief stricken to leave Ariadne behind. In his grief he forgot to change the sail from black to white. When Aegeus saw the ship returning with a black sail, he thought that Theseus was dead and in his grief he committed suicide by jumping into the sea. The sea is now called the Aegean Sea.

Pirithous

There are many other myths related to Theseus but another important one has to do with the abduction of Persephone. Theseus' best friend was Pirithous, another brave hero sired by Zeus. The two friends decided that since they were the sons of Zeus and Poseidon, they would marry Zeus' daughters. Theseus chose Helen. The two kidnapped her when she was still a child and left her with Theseus' mother Aethra with the plan that he would marry her once she grew up. The Dioscuri, Helen's brothers rescued her and kidnapped Aethra instead and made her Helen's slave for retribution.

During this time Theseus and Pirithous were on their way to the underworld to steal Persephone. Hades knew of their intentions but instead of fighting them openly he devised a shrewd plan. He pretended like he didn't know why they were there and invited them to a banquet. He offered them seats and once they sat on them, they couldn't rise back up because those seats were such that the person sitting on it forgot everything and never rose back.

Later Heracles rescued Theseus by raising him off the seat with his hand. He couldn't raise Pirithous though because Hades knew that he was the one who wanted to marry Persephone and held him back.

Phaedra

Phaedra was his second wife. She was the daughter of King Minos and she had two sons with Theseus, Demophon and Acamas. Acamas later was one of the heroes who hid in the Trojan Horse at Troy.

Phaedra was struck by Aphrodite to fall in love with Hippolytus, the son of Theseus by the Amazon queen Hippolyta. She did this because Hippolytus had scorned her by becoming the follower of Artemis instead of her. Phaedra couldn't believe how she could fall in love with her husband's son. It drove her crazy and she wrote a letter to Theseus, saying that Hippolytus had tried to rape her. Theseus killed Hippolytus in anger and when Phaedra heard this news, she killed herself because she had not wanted Hippolytus to die and she felt guilty.

Theseus was a generous king and gave away most of his power to the people of Athens and created a sort of democracy. But later on he lost popularity and was killed by Lycomedes who threw him off a cliff.

With this we finish the chapters on the heroes. There are many more myths about these heroes and even more heroes that we haven't mentioned. We have tried to cover all the interesting and important stories of the great heroes of Greek mythology. In the last chapter of this book, we'll look at some of the mythical creatures and beasts that inhabit the world of the Greek mythology.

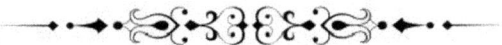

Chapter 14

The Beasts and Creatures

The Beasts and Creatures

The stories of the gods and heroes can't be complete without the beasts and creatures that they fought. The beasts are fantastically scary but the heroes always found a way to defeat them. Not all creatures were out to harm our heroes though. There were plenty of good creatures that helped the heroes in their quests. Without these fantastic beings, Greek mythology wouldn't be complete.

Cyclopes

The Cyclopes were the sons of Uranus and Gaia. They had only one round eye set in the middle of the forehead. They were born even before the Titans and were strong and powerful but Uranus found them to be monstrous. He banished them deep within the earth. This made Gaia deeply unhappy and she plotted to kill Uranus with the help of her children, the Titans.

The first three Cyclopes were Brontes, Steropes and Arges. They gave Zeus his thunderbolt when he released them from Tartarus. Since then there have been many Cyclopes in Greek mythology. Polyphemus was the Cyclops who Odysseus ran into during his journey back home. He was the son of Poseidon and Thoosa.

Centaurs

Centaurs were creatures that were half horse and half man. They had the upper body of a human and the lower body of a horse. Chiron was a famous centaur who was a teacher to many heroes.

Centaurs were said to be the children of Ixion and Nephele. Some sources say that they only had one son named Centaurus who mated with the Magnesian mares to produce the race of centaurs. Centaurus is also sometimes said to have been the son of Apollo and Stilbe. In this version, he also had a twin brother named Lapithes who was the ancestor of the Lapiths.

The myth goes that Lapiths and Centaurs were cousin races that were always fighting with each other. King of the Lapiths, Pirithous invited the centaurs to his wedding to Hippodamia but the centaurs got drunk and tried to abduct the bride and other Lapith women. In the ensuing battle, Theseus took the side of his friend Pirithous and destroyed the centaurs. This battle is known as the Centauromachy.

Greek mythology also had other creatures that were mixed with horses and it is worth mentioning them here. The Hippogriff was a creature that was half horse and half eagle. Hippocampus was the name of creatures that were horse from the waist up and fish from below. There was also a creature called the Hippalectryon which was half rooster and half horse.

Satyrs

Satyrs are creatures that were also half human and half horse but they were mostly human with equine features such as a horse tail and horse ears. Sometimes they were also shown as having an erect horse phallus. They were the companions of Dionysius and played flutes. The chief of the Satyrs was Silenus who was the teacher turned follower of Dionysius.

Later on, Satyrs were mixed with Roman Faunus, which were creatures that were half man and half goat and related to the god Pan. From then on, Satyrs were also shown as being half man and half goat instead of men having horse like features.

Giants

The giants were the children of Gaia and Uranus. Some sources say that they were born when Cronus castrated his father. The blood that fell on earth created the giants. Other sources say that they were the sons of Gaia and Tartarus. They are represented not as physically giant beings but normal human sized and human shaped beings that were born with armor and carried a spear, resembling the hoplites.

They weren't physical giants but were known for their strength and aggression. Their war with the Olympians is known as Gigantomachy. Some sources say that Gaia gave birth to them to take revenge from the Olympians for defeating the Titans. Others say that the giants tried to take over Olympus and it was their excessive pride and aggression that led to the war which destroyed them.

The myth goes that it was not possible for the gods alone to defeat them. They needed the help of a mortal and so Heracles helped them during the war. A lot of the giants were buried under huge mountains which then turned into volcanoes. A lot of existing volcanoes are said to have been born this way and the eruptions are said to be the result of the giants trying to escape from underneath.

Gorgons

The gorgons were dreadful female monsters in Greek mythology. The most popular of the gorgons were the three sisters, Stheno, Euryate and Medusa. Medusa was the only one that was mortal and Perseus killed her by cutting off her head.

The gorgons had snakes for hair and dreadful features including large bloodshot eyes and fangs. Anyone who looked at their face turned to stone. Athena also had the face of a gorgon on her shield as a device to fill her enemies with dread.

Typhon

Typhon was the scariest and most dangerous monster of the world of Greek mythology. He was the last son of Gaia. Tartarus was his father. He was shown as having a hundred heads and fire blazing from his eyes. Sometimes he's shown as having human form above the waist with wings and below the waist he has a snake's body. He was huge in size, with his head brushing the stars and had countless hands.

He was created by Gaia to destroy Zeus. He first ravaged the people of earth and destroyed most of the living things. He challenged Zeus but Zeus defeated him easily using his thunderbolt and lightning. He banished the defeated Typhon to the depths of Tartarus.

Typhon also gave birth to many children with the female monster Echidna. They bore the Lernaean Hydra, Cerberus the guard dog of Hades, Orthrus the two headed dog that guarded the cattle of Geryon as well as the Chimera. A lot of the later monsters and beasts were said to have been born by Typhon.

Hecatonchires

They were the children of Uranus and Gaia. They were born with a hundred hands and fifty heads. There were three of them: Briareos (the vigorous) who was also called Aegeaeon (the sea goat), Cottus (the striker of the furious) and Gyges (the big limbed).

They were personification of the wild forces of nature that caused earthquakes and typhoons. Uranus wasn't pleased by them and buried them deep within Gaia. They were later freed by Zeus and they helped him during the Titanomachy and were responsible for the final defeat of the Titans, as they were stronger than the Titans.

Cerberus

Cerberus was one of the children of Typhon and Echidna and is also known as the hound of Hades. He guards the underworld and prevents the dead from leaving. He is shown as having three or more heads and a serpent for a tail. He was one of the labors of Heracles where he was asked to fetch Cerberus by Eurystheus, king of Tiryns. Some accounts say that Heracles simply asked Hades for the dog and Hades said that he could take him if he could master the dog without the use of his weapons. Heracles subdued the dog using his lion skin as a shield. Heracles brought the dog to earth and paraded him through Greece before returning it to Hades.

Charybdis and Scylla

Charybdis and Scylla were two sea monsters that lived across from each other in a narrow strait. The strait was so narrow that the ships passing it were always in a dilemma. If they tried to escape one monster, they ended up getting too close to the other. This gave the rise to the idiom 'between Charybdis and Scylla' to mean to have to choose between two dangers. The Strait of Messina between Italy and Sicily is thought to have been this strait.

Charybdis was supposed to be the daughter of Poseidon and Gaia. She helped Poseidon during his feud with Zeus by swallowing islands into the water. Zeus was angered by this and turned her into a hideous monster with unquenchable thirst. So three times a day, Charybdis swallowed huge amounts of sea water, creating whirlpools that could swallow ships whole.

Scylla might have been a water nymph of great beauty. She made either Amphitrite or Circe jealous who turned her into a monster. From then on she would seize and destroy ships and kill all the crew.

Chimaera

Chimaera was a lioness with the head of a goat sticking out from its back. It also had a snake headed tail. It was said to be one of the children of Typhon and Echidna. It could breathe fire and was swift and strong. Chimaera was a female monster from Lycia. Bellerophon killed her with the help of Pegasus on the command of the Lycian king Iobates. Flying above her, he was immune to her attacks and shot her from the air with his arrows.

Hydra

Hydra was a multi-headed snake like monster with the special power that if one of the heads was cut off, two would grow back. This made her impossible to defeat. But Heracles found a way to defeat her. He went to her lair near the lake Lerna and threw flaming arrows into her lair to draw her out. He covered his nose and mouth to protect himself from her poisonous breath. He cut off her head but found that two more grew back. So he called his nephew Iolaus to help and Iolaus suggested that they burn her stump before new heads emerged. So Heracles would cut off her head and then Iolaus would cauterize the wound.

In this way Heracles was able to defeat Hydra. But Eurystheus argued that he had not completed this task on his own so he convinced him to do another task. This is one of the reasons why Heracles did 12 tasks when the original command was for 10 tasks. Heracles dipped his arrows in Hydra's blood after defeating her and used these poisonous arrows to defeat other enemies in his subsequent quests.

Pegasus

Pegasus is one of the most famous creatures of Greek mythology which is still a popular image among the people. He is a winged horse, completely white. It is said that he was born when Perseus beheaded Medusa. Her blood fell on earth and Pegasus and his brother Chrysaor were born. Pegasus flew to the heaven and Zeus tamed him and taught him to bring his thunder and lightning to him whenever he needed it.

Bellerophon was the hero who captured Pegasus. He used a golden bridle given to him by Athena to subdue Pegasus. Pegasus helped Bellerophon in many adventures but when he tried to fly to Olympus, he fell off the back of Pegasus and died. Zeus turned Pegasus into a constellation.

Phoenix

The Phoenix is another symbol from the world of Greek mythology that is still popular today. It is a large colorful bird that is reborn from its own ashes every time it dies. It is supposed to die in a large ball of fire and combustion and then rise from the ashes. The Phoenix is related to the sun and represents the son's journey, time and resurrection. Different accounts give different colors to this bird but every account agrees that it was so colorful that it was different from every other bird. It was slightly larger than an eagle.

Griffin

The griffin was a hybrid creature that had the hind quarter and hind legs and tail of a lion along with front talons, wings and head of an eagle. The griffin was known as the king of all creatures because it was a mixture of the lion, the king of all land animals, and the eagle, king of the birds. This symbol of the griffin existed in many cultures and was an important part of Greek mythology as well.

Python

Python was a huge serpent that was sent by Hera to chase Leto and stop her from giving birth to Apollo and Artemis on land. After his birth, Apollo took revenge from Python by chasing him to the oracle of Gaia at Delphi and killed it with his arrows. Later he built his own oracle at Delphi. In later versions Python is shown guarding the Omphalos, which was known as the mid point of earth, in the temple of Apollo.

Talos

Talos was a giant man made of bronze that protected Europa in Crete from invasion by circling the island three times every day and throwing huge rocks on any ship that approached the shores. Some myths suggest that Talos was made by Hephaestus at the request of Zeus. Hephaestus might have been helped by the Cyclopes as well. Other myths say that it was the architect/inventor Daedalus who made him.

Talos was strong and powerful but in most stories he is shown being defeated. When Jason and the Argonauts approached Crete, Talos attacked the ship. Medea was able to turn him insane with her magic and he removed a plug at his ankle and all the ichor ran out of him like molten lead, killing him instantly.

Charon

Charon is a character in the underworld of Hades. He is the ferryman who ferries souls of the dead across the river Styx and Acheron to bring them from the world of the living to the world of the dead. He is considered to be the son of Nyx, the primordial goddess of night and Erebus, the god of darkness.

The Greeks used to place a coin on or in the mouth of the dead to pay Charon the ferryman. Without a proper burial, the souls could not cross over to the underworld and were doomed to roam on the shore of the river for a hundred years. He is portrayed as an unkempt old man with a pole in one hand and sometimes with wide flashing eyes. In modern Greece Haros is used instead of Charon as the name of the ferryman.

Daemon

A daemon in Greek mythology was not similar to a demon as we know it today. A daemon was simply a nature spirit like a nymph. It was a benevolent spirit. For example the people of the Golden Age were turned into Daemons and they looked after later human races.

Nymphs

Nymphs are minor deities related to nature. They are depicted as young and beautiful maidens. They love to dance and sing and are freer than other women in Greek culture. They represent different aspects of nature.

There are many different types of nymphs based on the location that they reside in. There are Celestial Nymphs that reside in the sky among the gods, like Hyades and Pleiades. Land nymphs like Alseides and Leimakides reside on the earth. Wood and plant nymphs also existed. Anthousai were flower nymphs, Dryades were tree nymphs etc.

Then there were the water nymphs. Nereids were the daughters of Nereus and the sea nymphs. Naiads were the fresh water nymphs. Oceanids were the daughters of Oceanus and Tethys and were nymphs of salt water. There were underworld nymphs as well like Lampades, Orphne, Minthe etc.

Shade

Shades were also spirits or ghosts. But they were not divine beings. These are the most closely related to spirits as we understand them. When a person died, their shade could appear to others and tell them things. For example, Odysseus meets several shades in the underworld, including his mother's shade who tells him about the endless line of suitors for Penelope.

Geryon

Geryon was the giant who dwelt on the island Erytheia and who Heracles killed during one of his 12 labors, to steal his cattle. He was the grandson of Medusa. Some describe him as having one body and three heads. Others say that he had three bodies and one pair of legs. Yet more sources say that he had six hands and six legs and a pair of wings. He also carried a shield and a spear and looked like a fearsome warrior.

Harpies

Harpies were originally beautiful winged women who later turned into vicious birds with faces of women but with bent beaks. They were the daughters of Thaumas and Electra and the sisters of Iris. They punished people by stealing their food and also carried off those who had committed the sin of killing their kin and took them to the

Erinyes for receiving punishment. As mentioned earlier, they were torturing the old prophet Phineus when Jason and his Argonauts helped him to get rid of them.

Sirens

The Sirens were female creatures of incredible beauty and amazing voice. They sang and enchanted sailors to cause their ships to wreck at the rocky shores of their island. There are various stories about their origin.

The most popular one places them as companions of Persephone. When Persephone was abducted, Demeter gave them wings to search for her daughter. Another version says that they already had wings and when Hades kidnapped Persephone, Demeter took away their wings and cursed them to stay stuck on the island.

They are called the muses of the underworld. Their song is sweet but also sad and it ends with death. Some sources say that they were cannibals and drew sailors to their shores so they could eat them. Others say that they were just singing their songs and the sailors were drawn to them. They refused to leave the island and died of hunger because the Sirens couldn't feed them. They are numbered from 2 to 5 and described as beautiful maidens in earlier sources and later as ugly winged half bird half woman creatures like the Harpies.

These are some of the iconic beasts, monsters, hybrid animals and creatures from Greek mythology. Just like the gods and the heroes, the list of these creatures goes on forever. We've covered most of the important ones here.

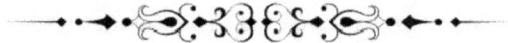

Conclusion

I want to thank you once again for downloading this book and hope you found it informative and interesting.

Greek mythology is a vast topic full of interesting tales and plot twists. Individual books can be written about each name mentioned in this book. So we've focused mainly on the first generation of Titans, the important Olympians and the famous heroes. We've also mentioned some other gods and divinities. The final chapter was about the beasts and creatures of Greek mythology. Even then we've only grazed the tip of the iceberg. More information and clarity can be obtained by referring to Greek classics like the Iliad by Homer.

We hope that you've enjoyed this book and have found the myths and stories interesting. We would be delighted if this book was able to develop a love for Greek mythology in your heart. We see many of these characters today in famous books and movies. The storytellers of our day continue to use these myths and these characters to tell entertaining and enlightening stories. This shows how powerful these myths really are. We suggest that you continue to dive deeper into this great ocean of knowledge and explore every myth deeply.

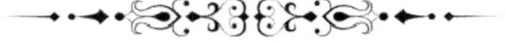

www.ingramcontent.com/pod-product-compliance
Lightning Source LLC
Chambersburg PA
CBHW051336170526
45166CB00002B/834